Crossing the
BRIDGE

Sharon Chase Hoseley

Printed in the United States of America.

Library of Congress Control Number: 2021910845

ISBN   Paperback   978-1-64803-804-4
              eBook   978-1-64803-805-1

Westwood Books Publishing LLC
11416 SW Aventino Drive
Port Saint Lucie, FL 34987

www.westwoodbookspublishing.com

Tom and pregnant Susan

"I owe much to God for giving me a strong mother and a loving father; for placing multitudes of influential people in my life as I was crossing my mother's safe bridge and for providing strong memories of life experiences."

I formed you in the womb and before you were born, I set you apart.

Jeremiah 1:5

Contents

Chapter 1

INTO THE WORLD WITH A BANG

Susan

"You won't mind if I get in some target practice while I wait?" Doc Carsow asks Tom as he climbs out of his shiny black car. He carries his black bag and a rolled-up bullseye. A pistol is strapped in his holster. "Got a competition this week. Need every chance to practice." Without waiting for an answer, he heads toward the empty hay field on our ten acres, sets up the target, then comes into the house to check on the progress.

"How's it going?" he inquires of Myrtle Mattoon, a nurse friend who's here to help deliver our baby.

"It'll be a while. Contractions are ten minutes apart," she reports.

"Good, good. Let me know when they're three minutes. I'll be out shooting." Doc lays a hand on my stomach for maybe a minute, then left.

What? I want to yell. I'm here. I'm having a baby. This is the most important day of my life and you don't care about anything but your shooting. But life's taught me that yelling solves nothing, so I concentrate on what's happening in my body. Pain increases—sharper and longer. By the time it calms down, I hear shots coming from Doc's gun.

Twelve years—Tom and I have waited twelve years. This baby's a miracle. Through starvation, freezing temperatures, scary attacks, lonely times, we've waited. Now this child's about to make our home complete.

"Bang . . .bang . . .bang." Shots ring from the hayfield

How can I be both excited and frightened? I know how to raise a child. At age eight, I looked after my baby sister, Edna, so Mama could work the farm. She didn't want much to do with girls. Girls were no good on a farm. Edna became my responsibility. I loved her and she loved me. We had each other.

"Bang, bang, bang."

Another pain begins. I concentrate on it, not sure what's happening or what I should do besides tell Myrtle. I grit my teeth and tighten my eyes. Whew! It's over. I talk to God; *I trust you. You know this baby inside me. Thanks for hearing my greatest heart-cry and years of tears. I want to be a wise Mama. Maybe I didn't do so good with Edna. Maybe I spoiled her too much. I was just a kid. I'll listen to you. I'll try to build a better bridge for this little one. I can't do this without you.* "Oh - ow - ow!" I cry out with an intense pain that sends shaking through my whole body. "Myrtle!"

"Bang, bang, bang." It's louder as she opens the back door and calls to the doctor. The shooting stops and the pain subsides. He stomps mud off his shoes before he comes in the door.

"Is everything ready?" he asks Myrtle.

"Yes, clean cloths, warm water, towels . . ."

I hear Doc wash his hands in our water bucket. He bursts into our small, one windowed bedroom. "It would help to have some light. Do you have a flashlight so we don't have to light a lantern?" I nod and our nurse hurries to find Tom. She rushes back with his small but trusty flashlight.

Suddenly the pain changes, and I know it's time. "Push . . . breathe . . . now push." He guides me. The pattern becomes more intense along with the pain until I barely have time to breathe. Suddenly I feel the baby slip from my body into the world. How amazing birth is! Our baby begins to cry as Myrtle cleans and wraps her in a warm receiving blanket made by my mama. What beautiful music that cry is to my ears.

Doc Carsow turns his attention back to me. While he works, he tells me quick instructions for taking care of myself and the baby. Then he washes his hands, packs his medical kit, his gun, and target and says, "Congratulations" and leaves. You might say our baby literally came into the world with a "bang."

Myrtle calls Tom in. He's been chopping wood to keep warm; to keep from going nuts. Men aren't good with things they can't control. I hear him stomp his feet and take off his jacket.

"Is she good? Is Susie all right?" he asks her. His next question is, "What is it?"

"A beautiful, healthy girl," she replies.

"Yahoo! Yes . . . yes . . . yes!" he yells as he breaks into the bedroom.

"Shh," I scold with a smile. "You'll scare her."

He picks up our little girl and cuddles her in his big, strong arms. "Hello, little Sharon," he whispers. "Do you know I love you?" He places her back at my breast to feed. He's glowing with pride. November 7, 1940, will be remembered as the best day of our lives.

Myrtle pulls out the bottom dresser drawer and places our sleeping baby on the soft blankets I prepared for her bed. It's just the right size. We'll have to make another sleeping place soon. Babies grow fast.

My sweet nurse hums in the kitchen. Tom leaves with his box of twenty-four cigars to share with the world the news that our baby girl has arrived. Of course, he'll smoke and brag a while before he returns. I think I'll take a nap.

*   *   *

Our Baby

Tom

I cain't tell you how I felt holdin' my baby in my arms. I wanted this from the day Susie and I got married. Twelve years, it's bin twelve years. I've a heap of guilt knowin' these years with no kids is my fault.

Paw said I was too dumb to learn. No more wastin' time in school. He made me his farmhand when I was nine. Guess he was right, 'cause I couldn't even do farmin' good. Every mistake deserved a beatin' . . .boards, chains, leather straps, whatever was handy. Thought sometimes he'd kill me.

When I was twelve, I couldn't stand the beatin's no more. I hired out to a neighbor farmer, slept in their barn. Went home on weekends. It was all right with Paw long as I gave him my pay. I'd take home part and leave the rest hid in the barn.

The outside marks healed good, but inside not so good. I think those beatin's did some damage that keeps me from bein' a daddy.

I know I'm no good . . . cain't do nothin' right. I try hard; I work hard, but I'm not good at much. If'n there's somethin' I can't solve or somebody tells me I'm wrong, I can't think what to say. Soos, I don't say nothin' for days, sometimes weeks, 'til I get it figured out. Don't wanna say it wrong.

Now, holding my baby . . . my little baby, lookin' at her purty face, I'm scared. I don't know how to be a daddy. Sure not gonna be like mine. Father, Paw, those are nasty words. I wanna be a daddy.

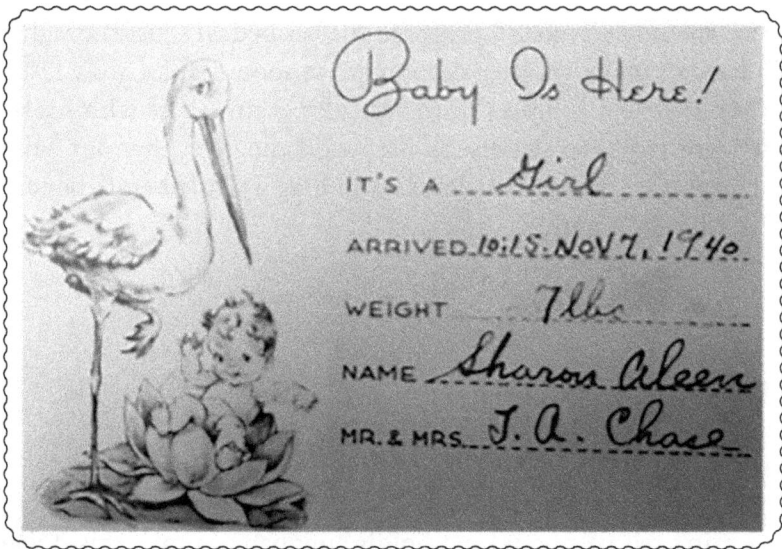

Baby announcement

Chapter 2

CONTENTMENT

Tom, Susan and Baby Sharon

Susan

Doc Carsow left a sheet of instructions:

> eat well,
> drink lots of fluids,
> don't lift over 10 pounds,
> bed rest for 2 weeks

Well, that's certainly easier than when Mama had Edna and me. She was on bed rest for a month and couldn't even lift a baby. I'll enjoy this pampering.

"Don't ya worry," Tom assures me as he kisses me goodbye on his way to work Tuesday morning. "Ya do what the doctor says. Get lots of rest and take care of the baby. I kin feed myself and make my lunch. Myrtle comes 'round eight ta check on ya and fix ya something to eat." He missed work yesterday just to make sure everything's okay. He's been like an old mother hen.

It's the third day and I decide to cook supper. Whew! I'm exhausted. I can tell it'll take a while for this thirty-year-old body to get back to normal. I get a good scolding from both Tom and Myrtle. The doctor was right. I need rest. I concentrate on following his rules. He's the doctor. He knows best. I must have patience.

My heart sings day and night with contentment for the first time in my life. My mind wanders back to my childhood frog friend. One summer I was filling the water bucket, and I coaxed a small green frog from the pond to be my friend. I made a bridge with my arm, quietly talked to him, and he hopped from the tall grass into my hand. That's all I wanted from my mama. I just wanted her to care about me, touch me, build a bridge between us. But Mama held no love for me. I was an interruption during gardening season. She was embarrassed and angry to be helpless at thirty-eight.

Only after I married did Mama say, "I love you," for the first time in my life. I proved worthy of her love by taking care of her when she had the influenza and nearly died. That won't happen to my little girl. She's going to know from the beginning she's loved.

Tom cuddles Sharon like she's the greatest treasure on earth. He wants at least six children. "We'll raise our young'uns right," he tells me when we talk about family. "We'll give 'em love we never got." Tom's mother loves him and he adores her, but his father's "a mean old cuss." We both agree we will never treat our children like that.

I pull my thoughts back to the present by a small cry . . . music to my ears, my dream come true. It says, "Mama, I'm sharing your bridge. I need you." I hold her, feed her, sing to her, rock her, talk to her. She'll always know I love her.

* * *

Today, our baby Chase is five days old. Myrtle comes bustling into the house with a plate of cookies. She makes coffee and sweeps the floor. "It's the day when baby and mama get to have visitors from the family," she says as she prepares to bathe Sharon. "What shall we dress her in?"

I reach in the top dresser drawer and pull out my baby dress; it's the only baby clothes I have besides the three gowns Mama made before Sharon arrived. The dress was hand-sewn for me by my Grandma Denney thirty years ago. It's worn, yellowed from years in storage, saved for this special day. I replaced the frayed ribbon and sewed up the torn button holes. She'll be beautiful in my dress.

"Now it's your turn." My nurse begins looking through my four dresses in the cardboard wardrobe. "What would you like to wear?"

I haven't thought about how I look. I've concentrated on the baby, living in my flannel gowns and barely running a comb through my hair.

"Would you like the blue dress or the blue dress or the blue dress or the blue dress?"

We both laugh. "Can you tell Tom likes blue?" I giggle. "He always goes with me to buy clothes and he says he likes the blue one best." I wash my face in the basin and wipe with a rag under my arms. We put thick cloth pads on each breast and bind it with a piece of old sheet to catch the overflow of milk. Myrtle helps me get into a blue dress with buttons down the front for easy feeding. She hands me a mirror and brush.

"Tackle your snarls. You know your own hair better than me," she commands as she hurries out to the living room to prepare for company. The tangles caused by six days in bed are a stinging reminder of my first haircut at age five. Mama cut off my long, beautiful, black curls because I couldn't comb them. I've kept it short. I need to wash it. Maybe I can tackle that job tomorrow.

* * *

I sit in the rocking chair and wait. Sharon sleeps in the dresser drawer pulled out and placed by the rocker.

Mama and Papa are the first to arrive. This seems so right. They should be the first to see their granddaughter. Mama comes through the door while Papa's getting something out of the back of the old, black, Model T.

"Oh, Susan. She's beautiful," Mama gushes.

I'm amazed. Mama would never have called Edna or me beautiful. Now her face shines with a broad smile as she bends over her sleeping granddaughter. Is it because she's old? Is it because her survival doesn't depend on this child? Is being a grandparent different from being a parent? Whatever the reason, it warms my heart to see her reaction.

Papa carries in four sections of a wooden structure and sits them next to the door. He stands silent, looking down at Sharon, gives me a big hug and says, "You're gonna be such a good mama to this little girl." My papa, always the encourager.

"We have a gift for her." He walks to the pieces of wood and fits them together. His best wood skills created just what we need—a crib. He hands Mama a bag, and she pulls out a handmade mattress and tucks it in the bottom. Our sweet girl has a perfect place to sleep with lots of room to grow.

Our baby wakes up. Papa reaches down and picks her up. "You've got your mama's black eyes." He whispers as he cuddles her close. He gives her a kiss on the forehead and hands her to Mama, who sits on the Davenport.

"Hello, little Sharon. Just look at that curl on the top of your head," Mama comments as she strokes her cheek. Sharon's dark eyes study her face. What a picture. My mama—showing affection to her granddaughter. Yes, there's been a change.

Myrtle brings cookies and coffee. The conversation is great, but the best part is, they love their granddaughter. My heart swells with joy to see my folks busting with pride over another baby in the family, even though it's a girl.

"We'd better go. Don't want you getting too tired." Papa starts toward the door. "I know Edna, Pete, and Patty are coming soon."

I hug the folks and whisper in my mind, *yes, all's right with the world. Thank you, Jesus.*

Chapter 3

LOST IN THE ONION SACK

Susan

I'm thankful for the crib. Sharon's growing fast. I don't remember my little sister changing this quick. I must make every minute count. Winter's been kind with only animal chores to do. Our ten acres and little house are paid for. We're in a good place to give our little girl love and security. As Tom would say, "We're snug as a bug in a rug."

The rain's washed away the snow. I love this time of year when new life's breaking out of its winter coat. The forsythia glows bright yellow in the front yard, the bridal wreath's budding. The six small shade trees in the front yard show signs of leaves and the fruit trees are forming buds. It'll soon be time to plant the garden. I'll put Sharon on a blanket, work the garden, and sing like my mama used to do. Even though our baby rolls over, she's figured out how to roll back onto the blanket. The fresh air will be healthy.

I finish doing the breakfast dishes and turn to pick up my daughter. "What?" I cry. "Sharon, where are you?" I run into the living room. My heart's pounding. How can she move so quick without me noticing? If she touches the wood stove . . . no, Sharon isn't in there. I dash back through the kitchen, through the enclosed back porch, and into the bedroom. Yes, that must be where she's gone. I look under the crib, under our bed, in our closet. No Sharon. How could she just disappear? What a terrible mother I am! I've lost my daughter, and she's not even crawling. I sob without breathing—terrified. "Get ahold of yourself," I tell myself out loud. "You've been in worse than this."

My sobs slow. I breathe deep. In the quiet of the moment, I hear the rustling of a sack and the thud of something dropped. I tiptoe to the door of the bedroom and look at the porch area. Sitting in the far corner next to the old cupboard where we keep pans for the milk separator is Sharon. She's into the sack of onions we brought up from the cellar yesterday, chomping away with her two little front teeth. Tears run down her cheeks. She spies me and her chubby little hands attempt to throw the onion as she laughs and says, "Ba, ba, ba." How many times have I rolled a ball to her and said, ball, ball, ball?"

I laugh. She scoots over to the onion saying, "Ba, ba, ba," picks it up and keeps gnawing. My baby flops on her tummy and elbows herself over to me. I'm still laughing as I put her in cousin Patty's wooden high chair, peel the rest of the onion, and give it back to her. She loves it.

Well, so much for putting her on a blanket while I'm gardening. I'll need another plan.

Sharon in baby buggy

*   *   *

Tom

Our marriage got off ta a bumpy road. Durin' the chivalry, Paw made a move on Susie. Was hopin' he'd not do that. All's I could say was, "Father likes purty young women." Hard ta explain, so's was silent for weeks. Most women would've left. Not Susie. Why'd she hang with me?

The depression sent us in deep stuff. No job, no home, no food, freezin' temps, days of silence 'cause I seen no way out. How'd she smile? Why'd she stick it out? I failed big time, not even providin' food or a roof ov'r our heads.

Gittin' on at the railroad was big. Steady money, paid for land, and came up snug as a bug in a rug. Yup! A good place. Don't have ta go silent much. Susie believes in me. Haf ta live up ta that. I done good fur once in ma life.

Chapter 4

A BOULDER HITS MY BRIDGE

Sharon standing by stroller

Susan

It's summer. Tom gets two weeks off the railroad. He drives grain truck for the McIntosh and Howard farms. This money goes into our savings. I hold down the fort weeding, hoeing, watering, and taking care of the animals. Our nine-month-old darling makes this a thrilling challenge. My sis, Edna, gave us Patty's stroller. Sharon loves to ride in her own "car." In fact, that was one of her first words, "Ka." I take her wherever I'm working.

"Come on, baby girl. It's time to feed the chickens and gather the eggs," I explain as I wheel her down the dirt path to the pen.

"Ka, ka, ka, ba ba, ma, ma," she chatters all the way. She loves animals and charms each in their language. Along with her babbles, she throws in giggles, makes faces and mimics their eating sounds. She's a great distraction while I milk old Betsy morning and evening. She entertains. I smile and thank God for my beautiful, healthy daughter.

* * *

Busyness makes time fly. Harvest is over. We leave Sharon to play with Grandma and Grandpa Kole one Saturday, borrow Papa's old Model T and go to Waha Mountain to cut wood for winter. That old crosscut-saw from our five years on the stick ranch still works just fine.

"We still have the knack. Sure glad we don't half ta cut another fifteen acres of these here trees," Tom exclaims as he wipes his brow.

"Me too," I pant. "Didn't realize I've gotten so weak."

"It weren't just cutting down trees back then. It was rocks, cold, snow, heat, no food. Man, how'd we survive?" Tom reminisces.

We become lost in our own hard memories as we saw away. There's a crack, a slow- motion crash, and an earth-shattering thud. We hack off branches and cut the thirty-foot trunk into stove length pieces. The bed of the pickup fills and we putt-putt the forty-five minutes to our house. Logs have to dry before splitting into stove wood. We spread them in a place where they're in the hot sun all day.

"We need at least five cords ta keep the cook stove and heater goin' through winter," Tom calculates. A cord's a stack four feet high, four feet wide and eight feet long. "That means at least three more trips. Hard work now—warm house later."

By the end of August, our cool dirt-cellar shelves under the house are full of beautiful jars of canned food. Our rented cold lockers at Knepper's store hold a cut up and wrapped pig and calf. Soon we'll harvest pumpkin and squash and dig root vegetables. Our cellar will be full. It's been a good year

* * *

It's time to split our winter heat supply. Tom chops; I stack it under the lean-to on the end of the chicken coup. We're almost finished with our third cord.

"I'm going in and start dinner," I tell Tom as I brush off my gloves. "Making chicken and dumplings from that fried chicken last night. I'll call when it's ready."

I stop by the apple tree where Sharon's playing in the dirt by the beehives.

"Come on, little girl," I say, "Let's go in and get some dinner. Are you hungry?" I brush off as much dirt as I can. She copies me by clapping her hands and laughing. She grabs my hand and takes tiny unsteady steps as we head to the house.

I replace my dirty work apron with a fresh one. We clean up in the white wash pan. Sharon yawns. I lay her in the crib, stoke the stove, and put a pot of water on its shiny black top.

The constant sound of hacking wood beats the contented song of a warm winter. Dinner's almost ready, table's set. "Susie . . . Susie . . .!" Tom's yelling startles me out of my daydreaming.

I open the screen and run screaming, "What Tom? What? What's happened?"

"Get rags—long ones. I've cut my leg!" He hollers back at me.

I spin around and dart to the house thinking, "What can I use? That old sheet I just tore up should work. Good thing I washed it. Oh, God please, please don't let this be bad."

As I rush into the bedroom and yank out the bottom dresser drawer, I notice Sharon's fallen asleep. "That's good," I say to myself as I grab an armful of cloth and tear out the door.

When I round the chicken coop to the chopping block, I nearly faint. Tom's curled on the ground, holding his blood-soaked pant leg. His ghost-white face and hazel eyes stare at me. He's shivering.

"I'm here, Sweety Pie." I hold my breath and take charge. "I'll wrap this tight around your leg, then you let go." Tom only nods.

I tie a long strip tight above the cut and wrap the shin wound as snug as I can. Blood soaks through as fast as I wrap, but it seems to be slowing.

"Let go. Lay back. Here, put your head on these." I shove the rest of the rags under his head. "I'm going to get help."

"Where, God. Where should I go?" Oh, I wish we had a phone. I wish I'd learned to drive. "Pop Daniels—he'll know what to do." I sprint my best quarter mile ever to the Daniels' house, pound on his door and shout, "Come quick. Tom's cut his leg." No questions. We jump in his car and race back. We find Tom curled where I left him.

"Here," Pop orders. "We're gonna get ya in the house. Put your arms cross our shoulders. No weight on that leg. Use us like crutches." All creation has stopped singing as we drag Tom to the house, up the stairs and into the screened porch. He passes out.

"Let him lay here. I'll get a blanket," I whisper, not wanting to wake Sharon. I fly into the bedroom, grab two blankets and a pillow. Scissors. I need to cut his pants leg, I think. By the time I come out, Pop has used his knife to slit the blood-soaked bandage and pants leg so we can see the cut.

The bleeding is slowing. Pink flesh lays open, revealing shiny white bone. I gag. My ears suddenly focus on the dumpling pot overflowing with a hiss. I jump to move it to the back of the stove.

"What now?" I ask. In all our years of survival, I've never dealt with anything like this.

"Turpentine," Pop replies. "Gotta clean it out and keep an infection away."

Tom's waking up. I grab the bottle from the kitchen cabinet and the wash pan. We put his leg across the pan and pour the liquid directly into the cut. Tom screams, "Ahhhiii!" and passes out again.

"I'm sorry, Tom. I'm sorry I have to hurt you more." I cry and pray as we pick out small wood chips from the cut and clean it again with turpentine. Pop pushes the cut together; I wrap it as tight as I can with long strips.

Tom's coming to. Pop speaks softly, "Tom, that's a real bad cut. I'll take you to the doctor."

Tom shakes his head, "No doctor. Never been ta one. Won't start now."

"It's bad," I plead. "Please, Tom. I could see bone." Tears pour down my cheeks, but my stubborn husband shakes his head. I know it won't do any good to argue with him. A boulder just hit my bridge.

*   *   *

Tom

Dumbest thing I ever done. I saw that knot in the log. Knew I shoulda sawed instead of choppin'. What good did all that cuttin' down pines do on the stick ranch if'n I didn't learn how to read the wood?

Here I am—leg chopped, useless, and silent. Susie keeps harpin' 'bout goin' ta the doctor. No sir, if'n I'm dumb 'nough ta cause this then I just haf'ta take my punishment. Suffer it out.

Chapter 5

HOSPITAL? NEVER BEEN HERE BEFORE

Susie

I doctor up Tom's cut as best I know how. My brother-in-law, Pete, brings crutches. My husband hobbles around the house, bumping into everything. He's never been crippled and thinks he can still operate normal. I can't keep him in bed. Such a persistent, hard-nosed man with no common sense! I clean the cut and put new cloth bandages on it every day. It seems to be growing new skin, but something's wrong. I can feel it, or rather, I can smell it.

On top of the wound, Tom's pulled into his silent treatment. He doesn't know how to handle this. For two weeks now, our house has been eerily quiet except for the chatter of little Sharon, the crackle of the fire, rain on the windows, and Tom's moans all night.

I can't take this much longer. Silently, I talk to my Rock. I know he'll never admit he's in a world of hurt. I once again rant at God. *Why God? Things were finally working so good for us. Why did you let this happen?* Hot tears pour down my cheeks and fall into my dishwater.

Gravel crunches in our driveway. I peek out the front door window and see Neen's shiny new black Model A. Tom's sister pulls hard on the handbrake and climbs out, slamming the door. She's recently gotten a nurse's aide job at the hospital in Clarkston.

"Thank God." I say out loud. "Maybe she can talk some sense into her brother." I yank open the door, run out in the rain, throw my arms around her and almost knock her over.

"Whoa," she cries. "That's the biggest welcome I ever received." She laughs. She backs up and holds me at arm's length. "Susie, what is wrong? Is Tom…?"

"He's stubborn, pig-headed, and something horrible's wrong." I blurt out.

"Oh, honey. I know. I'm a Chase. We can be mules. Sorry I haven't gotten here. Couldn't get a day off 'til I'd worked two weeks. These ten-hour shifts are killing me. S'pose I'll get used to it. Tell me what's goin' on." We walk slowly toward the house while I spill my fear and frustration on her ears.

As we step into the house Neen's eyes grow big. "Oh, my." She wrinkles her nose. "It stinks in here. Yuck! Tom, is that you that smells like a dead horse?"

"Now don't you start in on me too," Tom grouses. "Tisn't anything wrong time won't heal."

"Don't give me any sass, little brother," she shoots back. "That's not your everyday, you need a bath, odor. Remember, I just finished my practical nurse's training and I've seen that smell. Get your coat on. You're going to the hospital."

"Ya would pull that nurse thing on me, wouldn't ya," my husband counters.

"I'm not pulling a thing on you, Thomas Albert Chase. I'm saving your life. Now get your coat on," her voice raises two pitches.

I help him slip in one arm and then the other, get my coat, bundle up Sharon, and head out the door.

I whisper, "Thank you, Jesus, for making the sister as stubborn as the brother."

We load Tom in the passenger seat. I climb in the rumble seat and tuck our child under my coat to protect her from the wind, cold, and rain. Neen speeds off down Grelle, Thain, and Main street, pulling into White's Hospital in record time.

She runs in and comes out with a nurse and a wheelchair. Before I can get out of the back, they disappear through the door. Now I'm even more afraid. What's wrong that makes Neen behave like this?

As I enter the door, a woman at a desk rushes over to me. "You can't bring a child in the hospital," she commands. "Children carry diseases. These people are already sick enough. You must leave."

"But they just brought my husband in," I cry out. "I must see him."

"No children," she repeats. "Your husband's being well taken care of. You must leave."

That's what I do. I go to the car, crawl in the passenger seat and cry. Poor Sharon. She's confused. She reaches up and pats my wet cheeks. "Mama, Mama, Mama," she says over and over.

It seems like I've been sitting here for days. Cold penetrates the car. Frost forms on the inside of the windshield from our breath. Sharon falls asleep. I watch the hospital door for some sign of Neen or maybe a doctor. I shiver from head to toe. My head aches, my throat's sore from crying. Time has no substance or reality. All I know is, my Tom is somewhere in that building, maybe even dying, and I can't be with him.

The Voice from previous hard times floats into my mind. "Don't be afraid. I'm with you."

I heave a big sigh and shut my eyes. "Yes, I know. Thanks for reminding me." I whisper.

I wake to the door opening. "Oh, I must have fallen asleep." For a moment I forget where I am and why I'm here.

"They're doing surgery on Tom's leg right now," Neva states. "It's full of proud flesh. Poison. In medicine, we call it gangrene."

I suck in my breath with a whispered "No."

"You go in and wait," Neen advises. "I'll take Sharon home and come back later to see how things are going."

"They won't let a child in, even to see her own daddy." I'm chattering.

"I know," she sympathizes. "Hospital rules. Go 'long now. Your sweet babe will be just fine."

I stiffly crawl out of the car, place my sleeping baby in the seat, and head for the door.

As I open the door, I hear the car drive away and realize I didn't even tell Neen thanks.

*   *   *

I sit on a hard bench across from the woman who told me to leave. I know she was just doing her job, but being separated from Tom digs deep. During thirteen years of marriage, we've been through tough times; starvation, lumber jacking, poverty, depression, and isolation. We always did it together. I don't say a word to this busy looking lady. She doesn't even look up. I let my anger roll around inside my brain until my heart says, "Susan, give it up. I've got this."

I sigh and answer. I know. I'm feeling sorry for myself, and for Tom. I didn't realize how dependent we are, molded into one.

The unmoving hands on the clock let me know it's broken. How long has it been? The sun's making a retreat down the other side of the valley. I'm weary with worry, fear, and helplessness. I close my eyes.

They fly open when I feel a hand on my shoulder. It's Doc Carsow. "Susan?" he asks.

He doesn't remember me? Well, after all, it's been near a year. I nod my head.

"Tom's had a close call. The cut was full of slimy, poisoned puss. We call it gangrene. We opened the cut; cleaned it out, and treated it with sulfa. Another couple hours and we couldn't have saved his leg—maybe even his life."

"Oh," I suck in and can't say anymore.

"While we were in there, we found the small bone chopped clear in two. We set it. He has to stay off it until after the first of the year. It should heal okay now that we cleaned out the infection. Here's some pills for him to take when he goes home. We want to keep him here for at least a week. We can't cast it until the wound starts healing."

I manage to speak. "How long till…till he can go back to work?"

"We'll see. It depends on how fast it heals," Doc responds.

"If he can't work, I don't know how we can pay the hospital bill."

"Talk to that lady over there. She'll make arrangements for payments. Don't worry about it."

The lady who told me to leave? Not so sure about that.

"Tom should be coming out of the sedative. Would you like to visit him?" Doc asks.

"Of course, of course." I follow him down the hall.

Tom's in the middle of three beds in the room. He's snoring and pale. I stand staring at my husband I almost lost. I feel an overwhelming relief of thankfulness. Thanks, Jesus, for again taking us through a tough time. You know how much I need my Tom. Thank you, thank you, thank you. I blink back tears before I touch his arm. His beautiful hazel eyes slowly open and focus on my face.

"Susie," his hoarse voice whispers, "where am I?"

"In the hospital. Remember, Neen insisted you get help. You were mad. You need to apologize to her. She said you were raving all the way to town."

"Ah, I remember. What did they do?" He looks at his leg propped on a pillow.

I take a deep breath and tell the truth. "They cleaned out the gangrene, treated it with sulfa powder, and reset the small bone you chopped in two. Doc Carsow said another two hours and you would have lost your leg or maybe your life. Neen saved your life, Tom."

He was silent for a long time. "I was almost stubborn ta the end, huh? Should've listened."

"It's over now," I respond. "Be thankful for that. They're keeping you here until they see the cut healing with no poison."

"Here? In the hospital? No, can't do it." Tom tries to sit up. I gently push on his shoulder. "Money—cain't pay a hospital that long."

"I'll talk to the lady up front. It'll work out. You need to rest and get well. You can't go back to work 'til your leg's healed," I assure him. He relaxes. "I wish I could stay, but Neen has Sharon. I need to get home and tuck her in bed. I'll find someone to bring me back tomorrow. They won't let Sharon come. No kids are allowed in this place."

I kiss his forehead. My mouth smiles even though my heart's crying. "You rest and get well. That's your most important job right now."

"Susie, you're so good to me."

I smile, tiptoe out, and head to the front desk.

Chapter 6

WINTER HEALS

Tom on crutches with Susan

Susan

Winter sets in fast. The world sleeps under a white blanket while we heal inside and out. Good neighbors finish the wood pile. My family harvests the rest of the garden before the first hard freeze.

The railroad says they'll hold Tom's job open until he can work. It's a good time to get back on our feet. It'll be tight, but haven't we been here before?

Our little girl's turning a year old. Is that possible? She's our whole world. First birthdays are important. What can we give her? There's no money. War's tightened finances. Ration stamps are required for everything. With Tom not driving for a few months, we save our gasoline stamps and give them as gifts. But what would a one-year-old do with gasoline stamps? Maybe I can make something.

I open my old memory trunk. I pull out the long, brown, cotton stocking I hung every Christmas Eve. Christmas morning, it was filled with an orange from Uncle Martin who lived in California, some nuts, and a little hard candy.

Here's the brush I helped Papa paint the barn with when I was eight.

Tears fill my eyes as I lift out a small bag with a single black curl from the day Mama got angry and whacked off my hair.

A smile replaces tears as I open the sack holding my white lace chemise wedding dress. None of these things will work for a one-year-old.

My hand touches something soft. I pull out a handful of fur. Oh, no! It's the collar on my brown wool coat. My cousins and I bought them alike when we were seventeen.

I toss out school papers, drawings, books, and old dresses until I can see the coat on the bottom of the trunk. The moths have had a feast on the fur. What was I thinking? I should have put moth balls in there. I hold my breath and remove the coat, trying not to let fur fly. I gingerly shove the fur disaster into a paper sack, wad it up and put it next to our wood stove to burn.

"Now, let's have a look at the rest of the damage." I lift it out of the wooden trunk. "Oh dear, the bodice is so full of holes there's nothing I can do with it."

I unfold the dark brown wool. Well, the critters haven't nibbled the bottom section. There's plenty of good material there.

What can I do with it? I think. A teddy bear! I can make one like I saw in the store last Christmas. That's perfect for a one-year-old. I've heard they're named after our president, Teddy Roosevelt. I giggle. He looks like one with his sideburns and mustache.

I cut a pattern from a brown paper sack and lay it on the wide skirt of the coat. I stare at it for a long time. Got to have a picture in my mind before I start. It'll be easy with my sewing machine Tom gave me last Christmas. Stuffing? There's nothing soft and squishy. Too bad the fur's ruined. Maybe this old sheet.

I carefully fold it to just the right size for each of the pieces and sew each section together. I cut four arms, four legs, two heads, two bodies from the scratchy wool. Goodness, I've forgotten how wool feels. Hope it won't bother her. Oops! I sewed the body together before I attached the head. Oh, how I hate tearing out stitches! But it's got to be done right! Finally, I embroider eyes, nose and a crooked mouth. It doesn't look much like the ones in the store, but I make every stitch with love.

Company's coming Saturday. It'll be a tight fit in our tiny house. Tom's hand-cranking ice cream to go on my devil's food cake. He's been making ice cream often to use up the cream since we can't take it to the creamery in Lewiston.

Another reason I should have learned to drive.

My mama and papa come early. They're always first. Mama says, "If you're going someplace, gotta get there first so you don't have everybody starin' at ya."

Sharon yells, "Gamma! Gampa!" and runs to hug their legs. Papa swoops her up. She's twenty-three pounds now. At sixty his arms are still strong from trimming trees, berry bushes, and gardening. That's how they make their living: selling nuts, berries, and produce. It doesn't bring in much. They lost the farm and auctioned off everything. It was wise to buy a smaller place with only the two of them to carry the workload.

Papa's eyes sparkle. Mama leans in and tickles her granddaughter under the chin and makes clucking sounds.

"Look at what I made for your birthday, baby girl." She holds up a bright pink dress. "Let's put it on ya." She tugs off Sharon's dress and redresses her. "It's a little big, but she'll grow into it quickly."

Papa hands her a round package. "Tear off the paper and see what's in there," he says with a grin. "See, it's a ball inside a ball carved from cherry wood. When you move the outside ball, the inside moves another way. You don't throw this ball. You only roll it like this."

"Papa, that must have taken all year for you to carve!" I exclaim.
"Somethin' like that," he nods.

We sit and visit until we hear another car in the driveway.

"Hope that's not Alice," Mama snarls. "We had words yesterday. Don't wanna be in the same room with that nasty woman. Don't know why Johnny stays with her." She looks out the door window and smiles. "It's Edna, Pete, and little Patty."

Whew! I don't want any feuding at this party. It's supposed to be happy. Mama and my cousin Alice have been at it since my brother married her to get her away from her prostituting father. They lived with the folks for a while, stole all Mama and Papa's savings and ran away to California. The folks lost their farm. Boy, was Mama angry— still is. I don't think there's any forgiving going on.

Patty tumbles in the door. "Sharon!" she calls as she hugs her little cousin. They hold hands and jump around with little girl giggles. "Look," Patty says as she grabs a package from Edna's hands and jams it into her cousin's hands. "Open it, open it." It's wrapped in newspaper. Most gifts are, these days of war. Everything's scarce. Our one-year-old doesn't care. She loves tearing off the paper.

"I made the dress too big on purpose," Edna explains. "I remember how fast Patty grew at this age. That blue cup and plate set is made out of a new stuff they call celluloid. If it's dropped, it won't break like glass."

Our little house is full of happy sounds and heat. Sometimes that wood stove drives us right out of the house. The ice cream's becoming soup, so we open both the front and the back door. Ah, that's better.

Neen and Otis arrive with a warm sweater she's knitted. Grandma Chase brings winter stockings. Everyone's talking at once, so we don't hear the car drive in. The door opens. There stands Alice and Johnny. Mama's right, it's better to come early and not have everyone staring at you. The house shouts silence.

Mama jumps up and stomps out the back door. Papa follows, saying, "We've stayed too long." No one moves. We listen as their old car cranks up and drives away.

There's a collective sigh in the room. Alice shoves a gift wrapped in beautiful store-bought paper at Sharon. The paper's quickly ripped off, revealing a book and another dress—store bought. The chatter doesn't return. I'm glad they waited to come later.

One by one, our guests leave. I'm left with a sink full of dishes and a happy heart.

Sharon's asleep, worn out by her day of attention. My greatest thrill? She loves her teddy and took it to bed.

* * *

Tom

A week in the hospital and most loosin' the leg makes for deep thinkin'. Shoulda listened ta Susie. Stubborn Sis made me go. Now, I'm stuck in this rockin' chair. Cain't do much. Hurt my pride somethin' fierce when family and neighbors had ta get us ready for winter. Good it's winter tho, 'cause I couldn't stand not doin' my own spring work.

My happy thing is Sharon. We rock and sing. Smart little young'un. Knows my songs. Sings 'long. Love her giggles. She calls me Daddy. She knows my leg hurts, pats it careful like and says, "Poor leg," then comes 'long side the rockin' chair. I lift my little pumpkin on'a my lap. We sing, cuddle, take naps whiles Susie does chores. At least I kin watch 'er so's Susie gets jobs done. Now my Pumpkin's turned one. Love er ta death. She makes my upside-down life, good.

Sharon with teddy bear and doll and teddy bear

26

Chapter 7

1943

FREEDOM FROM FEAR

Susan

My greatest fear died today—Tom's father. I know I'm supposed to grieve, but it's a heavy load lifted from my mother-heart. He was a nasty, evil man, who beat his boys and abused his daughters as he would have me, if I hadn't hidden. I've harbored fear for my daughter since she was born. My heart sings thanks to God for protection and freedom.

Tom's humming. A new sparkle's in his eye, and his mouth curves slightly. It tells me he has the same reaction. The foreboding black fog of his family has lifted. The funeral will be a true celebration.

*   *   *

Tom

He's gone—that evil shadow what's haunted me since a child.

When we'd done our five years on the stick ranch, had only a week ta get outa our log cabin. That was the deal. Live free for five years if'n we cleared the pines.

Susie didn't complain eve'n when I moved us next ta Maw and Paw. Boy. Bad decision. I'd no idea how bad.

27

Father tried ta attack my Susie. Alone, no one fur miles. The dirty ol' cuss. I would'v killed him. She begged me not ta. Why'd he do that ta my wife?

Good thing my sis got 'im outta my sight. Never seen him since. I refuse ta go ta his funeral.

Chapter 8

LOOKING FOR HELP

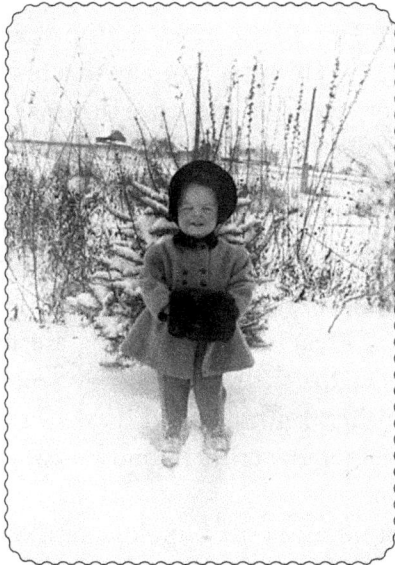

Sharon bundled up in the snow

Susan

Questions? There's always questions in my mind about being a good mother. I can't ask Mama because she was not a good mother. She demanded much from me. By the time I was five, I scrubbed clothes on a washboard, swept and hand-scrubbed wood floors spotless, weeded rows of baby radishes, and fed the chickens. I gathered eggs, picked berries, dried dishes, set the table for dinner and supper, and made beds. Mama kept me busy from the time I got up until bedtime.

I never met her expectations. I worked hard to win her approval, but not once did I feel a bridge of love and acceptance from her. I want to teach Sharon responsibility balanced with love. How do I do that?

These thoughts run through my mind again today as the cold January wind shoots through my threadbare coat and threatens to rip the scarf off my head. I blow on my knitted gloves to warm my hands, numb from carrying the metal slop bucket from the house to the pigpen. I shove the metal lid off the iron barrel and scoop two handfuls of oats into the discarded food and milk. Nothing ever goes to waste on a farm. There's always some critter needing what we can't eat. I let it set to soak up the liquid.

I glance down our alfalfa field at the house across the alley. Smoke's pouring out the chimney along with a few sparks—a sure sign someone just put more wood in the stove. Emma? No. Probably one of her older kids, or maybe her husband, Russell. He's a logger and can't work in winter. He's usually home November through March.

I chuckle to myself. Yup, there'll probably be another baby Snyder come again next fall. They've got seven now. Sure wish it was that easy for us. Looks like God's only gonna give us one.

Wait! Emma's a great mom. Her kids are hardworking, polite, and have deep respect for their mom. They seem to get along, have fun, and help each other. Emma? Yes, I'll ask her my questions. I turn toward the house, walk a few crunchy snow steps, then realize I hadn't dumped the bucket.

"Sorry. I forgot about you," I apologize to our sow as I pour the mush into her trough. "I was thinking about how to be a good mama. Something you don't have to worry about."

When Sharon wakes from her nap, I bundle us up and carry her through two-foot drifts to Snyder's little house. Russell built it on an "as needed basis" from reject lumber you get free at the mill. First the kitchen and eating area and a bedroom. As babies arrived, he added a bedroom for the boys: Ralph, Vernon, Raymond, and Gordon; then a bedroom for girls: Georgia, Alice, and Louise. Bunk beds line the walls. He built a living room last year.

"Knock, knock. Are you home?" I call out.

The door swings open as Emma welcomes me. "Susie, it's so good to see you. With all this snow, I'm going stir-crazy. Come in, come in." Two-year-old Gordon and five-year-old Raymond play on the living room floor with pieces of wood. Sharon joins them and I sit at the kitchen table.

"Russell's gone to get some oats for the cow. Others are still at school. Thank goodness for school busses. Can I get you some tea?" I nod. She grabs her best chipped cup, puts dried herbs in a sieve and pours boiling water through it from the kettle that's always on the stove, then sits herself down at the table across from me.

I stare at my cup and glance up and down the massive table covered with a red checked oil cloth and surrounded by long benches. Emma's only two years older than me. It's not the wisdom of age she can give me. It's the wisdom of experience. Where do I start?

"Um, Emma? I'm wondering if you can give me some advice on how to be a good Mama." There, I've said it. I let go of my pride and admitted I need help.

"Whoa! That's a loaded question, lady. I'm not an expert. I take one day at a time, handle each problem as it comes up, and pray a lot. I'm no perfect mom. Don't think anyone is."

I look up and smile. Hope I can stay as humble as Emma. "I know, but you've got experience. I want to know how you handle those problems. How do you get your kids to help with chores without being a dictator and making them hate you? I've watched your older kids. I can tell they love you."

"Okay." Emma takes a deep breath. "My thinking goes like this. Kids are people. They got feelings. They got needs. They copy me. That's how they learn. If I treat them with love and kindness, they treat me with love and kindness. If I respect and encourage them to do the best they can, they give that back to me. I ask, not demand. "Hugs go a long way too. It's not a perfect plan. Sometimes it turns upside down, but we try."

I shake my head. "Seems too simple."

Emma smiles. "Simple's a good plan. Love, be kind, respect and encourage. Give much, expect much."

I smile back. "I'm glad I asked."

Chapter 9

WHEAT FIELDS AND SUNDAY SCHOOL

Sharon in front of the farmer's shack

Susan

In '42 after Tom cut the bone in his leg chopping wood, he couldn't drive wheat truck for the McIntosh Farm. His leg's strong this year, and they're happy to have him back.

"Man, comin' home from the farm's the longest trip of my day." He complains the next morning. "Almost fell asleep on the road."

The farmer offers our family a one room shack during harvest. There's a water pump twenty feet from the door and a privy fifty feet beyond. Mrs. McIntosh's garden grows between their house and our shanty. To keep busy, I help pull weeds and pick vegetables. In return she shares them with us.

The smells of our temporary house bring back vivid memories of our log cabin on the stick ranch during the depression. At least it's better than the stinky, old, army tent we lived in for a year before we got that cabin built. Just thinking about that winter of minus fifteen degrees makes me shiver in the hot August sun.

Rattlesnakes are my biggest worry. Mostly they slither off when they hear us, but I wonder—would they do that with our almost three-year-old? Our busy girl is always exploring, picking up bugs, playing with sticks, trying to pump water, and jumping off the wooden steps.

It's Monday, wash day. I've scrubbed the clothes on my old wash board and I'm hanging them on the line, when I hear a squeal and see Sharon's plump little legs a blur as they race toward me. I sprint to meet her. "Mommy, mommy," she calls. "Look, look . . ." There's something cupped in her hands. My thoughts fly to a baby rattler. No, dear God. Keep her safe. Her wide smile tells me I have nothing to fear.

"Look, Mommy," Sharon pants. "It's nice and soft, but it's got stickers on its feet." She opens her chubby hands to reveal a tiny, frightened mouse who immediately hops off and runs through the stubble of weeds. We both laugh: delight on Sharon's part, relief on mine.

At the end of August, we return to our three-room house. It feels huge compared to our ten- by-ten hut on the farm. I feel like a kid again when I turn on the faucet and water gushes out. I'll never complain about having to tie cheese cloth on it in fall and spring to filter the mud. In the spring the cheesecloth has little fish and frogs when I take it off at night. Oh, but in the winter, the water is clear, cold and delicious.

"Thank you, God, that I don't have to pump water and carry the bucket. I'm grateful for my lumpy cotton mattress even though it sags from our weight. It's softer than the boards we've been sleeping on.

Thanks for my own garden which flourished under Pop Daniel's care. When I finish our harvest, we'll eat good this winter. We have a great life. Thank you."

*　　*　　*

Church

Tom

Huh! Susie's wantin ta take Sharon ta church. Only three. Too young. Besides, church is where people go and act all goodie, goodie. My father dun that. He was the devil the rest of the week. He made us say, "Our Father who art in heaven …" before supper every night. Didn't believe a word of it. If'n he learn how to be a father from Father God, I ain't havin' nothin' to do with church or God. Have ta be somethin' better. Soos, I tell Susie, "She's your youngun'. Take her if ya must. I'll have nuthin' to do with it."

Susan

Sharon's turning three in a month. She's still an only child. Our hearts ache to have another baby. It doesn't seem to be in God's plan. I can accept that. Tom loves his little girl, but is desperate for more children. His father beat him severely, in God's name, from the time he was nine years old. He said it was to make Tom work hard and do things right. Tom blames God for the beatings and not being able to have babies. He avoids the subject and wallows in his failure.

I'm ready to move on. I made a promise to teach Sharon about Jesus, and it's time I get more help with this task. I'm obviously not going to get it from Tom. I pray about this and work up my courage. On her third birthday, I approach my husband. "Tom," I begin, "before I got pregnant, I promised God I'd raise our child to be His child. I think it's time we get her in Sunday School."

There's silence—an extended silence I'm not sure how to handle. It's been months since I've received the silent treatment. I thought we'd moved past this. I guess not. We quietly pass each other over the next five days communicating only through Sharon. On the sixth day, Tom comes in from the evening milking, stomping the new fallen snow off his boots. He sits the milk bucket on the counter and says, "If that's what ya feel you half ta do, then she's your daughter. Ya take her. I won't have nuthin' to do with it." Tears spill into my dish water. I can't look at my husband because my heart's breaking for him. He's hurting and there's no way I can help.

The Orchards Community Church runs a bus. I call. They tell me to be at Twentieth and Grelle at nine on Sunday morning and they'll pick us up. Sharon and I climb on board the old yellow bus full of happy, noisy families. We're welcomed by smiling Don, the driver. It's happy for us too, yet there's an empty feeling. There should be three of us on this bus seat. *Oh, God, I wish Tom was with us.*

*   *   *

Daddy's Little Girl

It's not that Tom doesn't love Sharon. I've never seen a more devoted dad. Even when his leg was healing, he'd sit in the big homemade rocker, lift her from the side onto his lap, wrap her in his big strong arms and sing to her.

"Come on, Pumpkin. It's rockin' and singin' time," he calls. I think their cuddle time will only stop when she's too big for his lap.

> "Oh, I went down South for to see my Sal,
> Sing Polly Wolly Doodle all the day;
> Oh my Sal, she am a spunky gal,
> Singing Polly Wolly Doodle all the day.
>
> Fare thee well, fare thee well,
> Fare thee well, my fairy fay
> For I'm goin' to Louisiana, for to see my Susi-anna,
> Sing Polly Wolly Doodle all the day."

Our little girl giggles, reaches up and pats Tom's face and pleads "More, Daddy. More"

> "Oh, it ain't gonna rain no more, no more
> It ain't gonna rain no more.
> How in the heck can I wash my neck
> If it ain't gonna rain no more?"

"Froggie, froggie," Sharon demands. It's her favorite, and at three years old she can sing all ten verses along with her Daddy.

> Froggie went a courtin' he did go, uh-huh, uh-huh
> Froggie went a courtin' he did go, uh-huh…"

They sing at the top of their voice and clap along. Oh, it makes me feel warm and happy inside. Rocking and singing; what beautiful memories they're making. Tom's beautiful tenor voice rings with delight. They're getting louder and louder. Tom rocks harder and harder. Hope the neighbors don't mind. I'm sure Mrs. McMillan can hear them over by the raspberry patch.

CRASH!

"Tom, Tom," I cry and run into the living room. "What hap . . ." There's silence as I try to collect my thoughts. The rocking chair is upside down. I only see Tom's feet sticking over the front edge. "Tom!" I scream. "Are you okay? Is Sharon hurt?" There's still silence and then I hear little girl giggles someplace in the corner behind the tipped over chair.

"Again, Daddy, again. That was fun. Do again." Tom's chuckles turn to out-loud laughing. I join them, relieved that everyone's all right. The big puzzle is: how to get them out of the rocking chair corner jail.

Chapter 10

AIRPLANE FEARS

Susan

The war's drug on forever. It's been going on my daughter's whole life. It's hard. Sugar, salt, flour, gasoline, and spices are rationed. We pick up our ration stamps the first of every month at the court house. When they're gone, we can't buy those things 'til next month. Sure am glad we live on a farm and grow most of our own food. It will be nice to put sugar in my canned fruit and make jam and jelly again. But that's a small complaint. It must be hard for city folks who have to buy all their food.

When our cow's dry, we buy something called oleo margarine. It looks like a big block of lard. It comes with a pack of yellow dye to work into the white to make it look like butter. It may look like it but it doesn't taste like it. From the time Sharon could stand on a chair, she's mixed the yellow and white. She loves the feel and the idea that she's "cooking."

It's gasoline where we have to be careful. It's a long walk for Tom to go to work if we run out of gas. On Saturdays the gas lines are long. Sometimes it takes two hours to fill the tank. Gas stations aren't open on Sundays. Neither are stores. It's totally a day of rest except for people like Tom who work on the railroad. He and Everett Leachman take turns driving down Lindsey Creek to the Camas Prairie Railroad Yards when they're on the same shift. Helps both of us conserve gas.

We understand this war's important. Evil people have done horrible things to good people. Tom was too old for the draft. We support our country by sending packages to service men. We even bought two savings bonds for Sharon. If she keeps them 'til she's twenty they'll be worth fifty dollars. That's a lot of money. Meantime, Uncle Sam uses the money to fight the war. Our sacrifices are small compared to the men who are in the fight.

The hardest thing is Sharon's fear of the Fairchild Air Force Base bombers practicing in the sky above Lewiston. We have to take some blame for it. Every night, Tom and I listen to the President's fire side chats. He talks about planes, bombs, dog fights in the air, people dying— probably stuff our little girl shouldn't be hearing. If we don't listen, we won't know what's happening in the war. We didn't think she would understand.

Planes drone over the valley three to four times a day. Sharon runs into the house screaming and hides. Sometimes they fly high; sometimes low enough to shake the windows. You'd think they're trying to unnerve their own citizens. It terrifies our sweetheart.

Tom's cousin, Leo, knows how to fly a plane. He helps us make a plan to calm her fears.

Maybe it will work; maybe it'll make it worse. We've got to give it a try.

*   *   *

Sharon

"Look! a fish. And a Schmoo." I point my chubby finger at the fluffy white cloud that looks like my favorite thing from Lil' Abner in the funny paper. "I like Schmoos. They taste like chicken and always come back to life. Can I have a Schmoo?" I turn my head toward Mama lying on the blanket beside me on our front lawn. She smiles.

It's summer, 1944. Imagining cotton-cloud pictures in the blue sky is our favorite thing. Mama canned apricots on our black wood stove this morning. The house is like an oven when Mama cans. It's so hot, I put the butter in the ice box in the dirt cellar or it'll run all over the table. We cool off in the shade of the cottonwood trees. The thin blanket soaks up the water left on the grass from the sprinkler this morning. It feels good, but not as good as when I run through the sprinkler.

"Close your eyes and listen," Mama suggests. "What do you hear?" I shut my eyes tight and listen with both ears.

"A honey bee! Buzzzzzzzzz." I mimic my favorite little critters from the hives under the apple tree. I play with my cars in the dirt around their houses. They're always busy. Come and go, come and go. When it gets cooler, Daddy dresses up in white with a big hood. He lights a little fire in a thing that looks like a coffee pot with a pump on the end. He says the smoke makes bees go to sleep so they don't get mad at him when he robs the hive. I didn't like that he robbed them, but he showed me he doesn't take all their honey. He leaves enough for them to eat in winter. I decided this kind of robbing is all right. I love honeycomb. You can chew the wax a long time after the honey's gone. I had gum once. Honeycomb's better. Mama cuts the comb off the frame and wires and puts it into a big pot. She cooks it slow. The honey melts and the comb floats to the top. Then she puts it in jars for winter. It makes the house smell yummy.

"Bees are our friends, you know."

"I know. I hear some birds singing." Mama adds. "Do you know what kind of bird that is?"

"Nope."

"It's a robin. Those big gray birds with an orange breast?"

"The ones pulling out worms?

"They eat worms and berries."

"Tweet, tweet, tweet . . . tweet, tweet. I can talk bee and robin."

We both laugh.

My bird tweeting stops at a distant rumbling in the sky. The sound makes me shake. "No," I scream. "Run, run. The bombs are coming. The bombs are coming!" Before Mama can touch me, I streak into the house. I scream from under my bed. "Hide Mama. Hide!"

Mama's callous hand strokes my trembling arm as she reaches into the dark. "It's all right, honey. The pilots are just practicing. They won't bomb us." She hums, "Hush little baby, don't say a word . . ."

I'm not sure about that. The president talks on the radio every night about war. He says planes bomb. Planes fight. Planes crash. I'm afraid of planes. They growl across our pretty white clouds and sound like they want to eat us.

"Listen," Mama whispers. "The plane's gone. We can't hear it now. Come out."

I lie still and listen. No, I can't hear the monster. I creep from under the metal frame. Mama holds me tight. I'm always safe in Mama's arms.

*　*　*

Sharon

Mama takes me by the hand and leads me to the middle of our driveway. I'm wearing a red polka dot dress—my favorite. I put it on because Mama says we're going somewhere special. This doesn't seem special. We're just standing here, in the driveway, in the sun.

"Mama, I'm hot," I complain and curl my bare toes into the gravel.

"Let's stand in the shade for a minute," Mama suggests.

"What are we standing here for?" I asked impatiently as I hop to the cool green grass.

"We must wait for the surprise."

A surprise? Maybe I'm going to get an ice cream from the grocery truck that comes by our house. That'd be nice on a hot day. Or, maybe, Patty's going to visit. I love my cousin. They live a long way and don't come much. Waiting's hard. Especially when you don't know what you're waiting for. I stand on one foot and then the other while Mama holds my hand.

After forever, I freeze to a sound coming in the sky. I try to pull my hand from Mama's. She holds tight. I try to run. She pulls me to her.

Her soft voice says, "Sharon, look. Look up in the sky. See that plane? Watch closely. It's going to come right over us." She's kneeling beside me now with her arm around my red and white polka dots as she points up.

I quit struggling and raise my head. It's a little plane, coming closer and closer, lower and lower. I'm frozen. That happens sometimes when I get afraid. I see people, two of them, in the plane. One of them is waving . . . it's my . . . it's my daddy! My daddy is in that plane and he's waving at me.

"Hi, Daddy!" I yell and bounce up and down. I watch the plane go away and make a big circle in the sky. "He's coming back." I'm dancing up and down the drive. Lower and lower it falls until I can see Daddy again. We wave hard and he blows me a kiss. I blow back. "That's my daddy. He's flying!" I hug Mama and she hugs me. The plane sound goes far away.

"Planes are good." Mama whispers in my ear. "Some are little and some are big, but planes are good."

"Yup, planes are good." I whisper back.

*   *   *

Tom

Sharon's scart ta death of planes goin' over. We listen ta the news 'bout the war, the President's fireside chats, and read the paper with all kinda stories 'bout planes bombin', crashin', fightin'. Susie and I decide this ain't good.

My cuzin, Leo, flies. I made him a deal. I'd pay fur the gas if'n he'd fly over our house some. I'd wave at my little pumpkin. Maybe she'd get the notion not all planes are bad.

I tell you; I was scart ta death too. Never been up in one of them contraptions. It took all the courage I had. I shook so bad when I got in that plane. Once we was up there, twern't so bad. Leo told me he'd "buzz" the house two times. That means, he'd go low enough she could see me.

I smiled and wave hard both times. I seen her in the driveway jumpin' up and down. That made my heart jump too. It done me good ta see her so excited.

When we landed at the air-o-port, I blew a big breath. Didn't know I'd been holdin' it all that time. Not so keen on doin' that agin.

41

Chapter 11

THEN COMES WINTER

Sharon

My birthday begins a lot of celebrations: my birthday, Thanksgiving, Grandma's birthday, Cousin Clifford's birthday, then the best of all, Christmas.

Christmas Sunday night. I wear my new, rose colored taffeta dress from Grandma and Grandpa. Excitement tickles so much in my five-year-old tummy, I can't even think 'bout eating. The drive to the church is forever, the long white costume and wings cover my pretty dress. It's hot, hot, hot next to the ceiling. But nothing keeps me from singing out my first song all by myself, cause I'm the angel on top of the kids' Living Christmas Tree. "There's a song in the air, there's a star in the sky . . ."

Maxine, the director, says, "Sharon, that was beautiful. You sang like an angel."

I giggle. "That's 'cause I am an angel."

I can tell Mama and Daddy like it by the way they hug me and say they're proud of me. It's the first time my daddy's ever come to church. I'm glad he likes it. Maybe he'll come back.

Chapter 12

AUGUST 5, 1945

A GREAT CELEBRATION

Susan

An invitation came in the mail today: "You're invited to celebrate George's 40th birthday. August 14, 6:00 p.m. at the Haskin's house on Lindsey Creek Road. Meat will be grilled. Bring a side dish, a small funny gift and your instruments. It's a SURPRISE."

Ooh, this will be fun. George is married to my cousin, Mae. They have two boys, Don and Larry. Don has diabetes. He's sick a lot. It's hard to get a teen to eat right. Larry's seven years older than Sharon and loves her like a little sister. We get together often, play cards, and visit. Tom turned forty in February, but he didn't want a party.

Hmm, what shall we get for a gift? Tom will think of something.

Neither of us play instruments, but we love to sing. Music's a part of family get togethers—Friday night jams, dinners, weddings, birthday parties, and even after funerals. That seems strange to me; singing and playing all night after we cried for our loved one for two hours.

It's toe-tappin' stuff, but no dancing like I did growing up on the prairie. No, these folks have found the Lord, and dancing is of the devil. I'm not sure where they get this. I remember that King David danced in the streets when he was celebrating. What's wrong with it? Dancing's absolutely forbidden in Tom's family. You'd think Tom, not

43

being a believer, would pooh-pooh this idea, but he's the worst. He once told me, "No daughter of mine's ever going to dance." We sing along, tap our toes, and clap our hands. Oh yes, and eat. That's the other thing our families are good at.

*   *   *

Sharon

"Wear the brown dress with little flowers Grandma made you," Mama tells me. "You'll be playing outside. The dirt won't show so much."

I take it out of my clothes box where Mama folded it all nice after she ironed it. It's summer, so I wear anklets and not those long, brown, winter stockings I hate.

Mama makes her famous potato salad. She always makes two—one with onions and one without. Some people don't want onions. How can you not like onions?

"It's time," Daddy calls. We pile in the car with me in the middle. I get to hold the present. I can't tell anyone what it is. I say it over in my mind. It's a wooden nickel like stores give. When you get twenty you get to spend it. It's funny, and he can buy stuff with it.

"Oh, this is a big party!" I exclaim as we arrive at their place. "Look at all the kids."

George runs to our car. "Good to see you, Tom and Susie. Sharon, my favorite little girl. How are you?" He lifts me high in the air and I giggle.

"Here, this is for you." I push the box in his face. He puts me down, takes the box and kisses my forehead.

"Why thank you," he says with a big grin. "I wonder what's in it?"

"I can't tell. It's a surprise," I affirm, "surprise, surprise, surprise."

Here comes Larry. He takes my hand and we go play Kick the Can in the side yard. We're on the same team. You're s'pose to get the can to the line on the other side of the yard, but can't touch it with hands, just your feet. Everyone's kicking at the same time. The other team's trying to stop us. Larry doesn't let big kids run over me.

"Ouch," I cry out. "Jack just kicked my knee." Well, I guess he can't protect me all the time. I hear screams and see Larry kick the can across the line.

"Yea! for Larry," I yell.

"Can races," Larry shouts. "If you're under six, line up on this side."

The winner always gets to choose the next game. There's five of us under-sixes.

"Here's a can for each of you. When I say 'Go,' you have to kick your can to the other line, but it can't leave the ground. It's gotta stay on the ground. First one to kick the can across the finish line wins."

I can do this, I think.

"Ready, set, GO," Larry yells.

I learn real quick to kick the can's side so it rolls. If you kick the end it doesn't go the right way. Oops. mine almost left the ground. Slow down, kick the side, roll it. John and Patty are ahead of me. Got to hurry. John gives a big kick—too big. It leaves the ground, the grass, and goes in the flower bed. Slow down, kick the side, roll it. I'm gaining on Patty. Almost there, kick the side, roll it and my can goes over before Patty's. I grab my can and hold it in the air. Everyone's cheering, "Winner, winner, winner."

"Hot potato," I call out. We sit in a circle on the grass. I pass the can to the next person calling out "Hot Potato." If they drop it, they're out of the game. You can't hang onto it or you get burned. You have to say "Hot Potato" and get rid of it. If the passer doesn't do a good pass, he's out. The last person in the circle wins.

James wins just as George rings the big bell by the front door and hollers, "Meat's done!"

Uncle Willie says grace. We don't do that at home 'cause Daddy doesn't like talking to God. Grace is when you ask God to bless the food and the people who brought it. Uncle Willie ends with, "And Lord would you please put a stop to the fighting and this war. We're getting mighty tired of it. Thank you."

There's a loud, "Amen."

Big tables are in the front yard. I mean, they're three sawhorses long. Boards go from one end to the other. Benches too, boards on stumps. One table's got food. The others are for big people. We kids sit on the ground in the shade of a tree. Big people go first. It's the polite thing to do. Besides, then we kids can take all we want.

Mama reminds me, "You can help yourself, but remember, you have to eat all you take or there won't be birthday cake later."

A large half barrel sits on metal legs with mesh wire stretched over the top. It smells like roasted meat and makes my stomach rumble. Oh, my, what the women in our family can make from home grown stuff: corn on the cob, fruit salads, green salads, coleslaw, potato salad, baby potatoes, berry cobblers, and even biscuits. I stuff myself.

George opens his funny gifts. We tease and laugh. He gets fifteen wooden nickels. The men gather at one sawhorse table to smoke and play cards; the women go wash the dishes. Larry and Don bring out crayons and coloring books for us kids.

*　　*　　*

Susan

I'm helping Mae finish up the dishes when she stops and looks at the refrigerator.

"You know, I don't think there's enough ice cream. More people showed up than I figured. Maybe I'd better have George go to town and get more before Huggin's closes at nine. Thank goodness the creamery stays open so farmers can get their cans in from night milking. George, George," she calls as she goes through the door.

A few minutes later I hear our car start up, look out to see Tom and George headed out.

"Whew," Mae exclaims. "Glad I thought of that. What's cake without ice cream?"

With the dishes done, we sit and visit, waiting for ice cream. The noise of the party dies down. Even the kids color quietly at a table.

Strange sounds invade the warm August evening. A jumble of noises come from far away: whistles blow, sirens scream, gunshots and loud booms echo off the hills, church bells clang. It gets louder and louder. What's going on? My heart leaps into my throat. Are we being attacked? We vault to our feet and freeze in confusion and fear. The clamor comes from Lewiston, five miles away. So harsh, so unnerving, so…petrifying. Has the war reached us?

In the silent yard, Sharon scoots over to me. I wrap my arms around her, pull her close. I feel her heart thumping hard and know she's reliving her fear of bombers. I whisper in her ear, "It's all right, honey. God's here to protect us." I listen, wonder, pray, swallow my fear and fight to bring my faith to the front of my mind. Tom's there in Lewiston. Jesus, keep him safe. Bring him back to us.

As if God gives immediate answer to my prayer, our car roars into the driveway. George jumps out yelling, "The war's over, the war's over!"

Mae looks sternly at her husband, "George Haskins, don't you joke about that. It's not a thing to be joked about."

"It's true, it's true," Tom chimes in. "Listen you guys. Listen ta Lewiston celebrating. The Japanese have surrendered."

The yard erupts in cheers. Tears stream down our faces. Everyone hugs and shouts thanks to God, screams with astonishment, jumps for joy and yes, even some dancing happens. How can you not dance with such good news? Instruments appear and we begin to sing at the top of our lungs, "God bless America, land that I love …"

Cake and ice cream for everyone. We celebrate, not just a birthday, but victory over evil. It's never tasted so good.

Chapter 13

PROTECTED AND RESCUED

The Chase's home

Susan

I love our place in the Orchards. God had this place picked out for us all along. He moved us to Clarkston, a ranch, a musty old army tent, a log cabin, a house on the river with ice flows, threatening flood waters, and my scary father-in-law next door. Now God's settled us on these ten acres of fertile land, and we're content. Six moves in twelve years—

one of those years spent in a tent in fifteen below zero; four in a log cabin. It's all behind us.

We're comfortable. Good land, a safe neighborhood, and even though our little one- bedroom shack is a bit small for three people, we're doing well. It's paid for! Sharon can explore and discover, play and have friends, learn responsibility and grow up safe.

Tom's wrapped his life around our little girl. He works hard at the railroad and at keeping our little farm in shape. He includes Sharon in his chores. His day always ends cuddling her in the big rocker.

"What's the most exciting thing you did today?" he asks.

"I picked fat green worms off the tomato plants." Sharon giggles. "Do you know that they feel soft and squishy like where you get milk from the cow?"

"Hmm," Tom answers. "Never thought of that. I guess you're right."

They discuss all kinds of things until she yawns and says, "Daddy, I'm sort of tired."

They do their ritual of washing hands and face and brushing teeth. Tom carries her to the cot in our bedroom and gives her a kiss. I help her into her gown and say prayers with her. Sleep takes her away immediately.

Sometimes her exploring gets her in a pickle of trouble. I know she'll learn by experience. I trust Jesus to protect her.

*   *   *

Rescued Sharon

We live in a big, big place. It takes me all day to go everywhere in it. I'm the watcher, you know. I can tell you where all the holes are in the alfalfa field. Daddy says they're made by gophers. I don't think he likes them. Maybe because he stepped in one when he was putting hay on the wagon and hurt his leg with the big scar.

That field has flowers too. We don't even plant them. There's purple ones and tiny, little blue ones and round puffy yellow ones. I pick a bouquet for Mama every day. She puts them in a jelly jar. I think she likes them.

At the bottom of the alfalfa is the pigpen. Daddy tells me, "Don't get in there 'cause pigs can be mean." Look at that fence. I tug on it. It feels strong. Pigs can't get out. I climb up the fence and sit on top. Pigs are sure funny lookin'. Big fat body, tiny legs, flat nose, teeny eyes and big floppy ears.

I laugh at them. "I can be taller than you," I yelled at them. "Just watch." I grab the fence post and stand on top of the fence. "See, I'm bigger than you." I start walking on top of the boards. "Whoopee! This is fun. You can't do this" I yell at the sow lying in the mud.

The board under my next step slips sideways and falls off. So do I. Wham! Right into the pigpen. The cut off stem of a pigweed rams itself up my nose. I'm shocked. Blood is squirting out; I can't breathe. "Oh, no. The pigs are gonna get me for sure."

It dawns on me: yell, Sharon, yell! "Help, help!" Every time I open my mouth, it fills with the blood spurting from my nose. What am I gonna do?

"What's going on?" I hear. I look up and see Vernon, the Snyder's big son climbing into the pen. He picks me up, climbs out, and carries me to my house.

"You know you shouldn't be playing in the pigpen." he scolds. "It's not safe. You scared me to death with this blood all over you. I thought sure the pigs got you."

He pounds on our back door. Mama looks scared. "She was playing in the pigpen," he tells her. "I was working in the garden and heard her. Hope she's okay." He heads back home and Mama hustles me to the kitchen.

I want to tell her, "No, I wasn't playing in the pigpen," but something about her face says keep quiet. She wipes my face, hands and arms with a cold, wet rag. Blood is still running from my nose. She tips my head back. Yuck, the blood starts running down my throat. I think I'm gonna vomit. The drizzle stops and she lets my head up.

"Tell me what happened." She asks in a quiet, shaky voice. I tell her the truth—the whole truth and repeat it over and over, "I wasn't playing in the pigpen. I was walking on the fence." She gives me a big hug for a long time. Maybe I'll have to help Daddy build a better fence.

*　　*　　*

I love playing cars in the dirt under the apple tree. That's where the bees live too. They keep me company but won't let me touch them. This morning the bees are up in the tree because there's flowers up there. Daddy says they make honey out of the yellow stuff in the flowers.

I have three cars Grandpa carved for me. The wheels don't move so they make deep trails. The big one makes a big, big road. Oh, what was that? Something hard in the dirt won't let my car go. I'll dig it out with a stick. Here's a big one. Hm. That thing's short and shiny. Look, it's a pocket knife like Daddy's.

Oh, goody. Now I can carve something like Grandpa does. Hm. How do I get it open? Grandpa just pulls on it. Oh, I see the knife part. Pull, pull, pull. It's stuck. Pull again. It's so dirty. It can't get open with all that dirt on it.

I scrape off more dirt. I pull hard and whack—the knife flies open and right into my skin between my thumb and finger. Oh, no. I squeeze the skin together with my other hand because it's starting to bleed. If I squeeze hard enough it will go back together and Mama will never know I was playing with a knife. I squeeze and squeeze and squeeze. It works for a little bit, but every time I let go it bleeds. How long does it take to go back together? If it takes all day, I won't get any dinner.

After all the blood in the pig pen, I wonder how much I have left. Maybe I can just walk in the back door and sit at the table and Mama won't notice. Oh, dear, I hear Daddy's car. Daddy always comes to the back door to take off his boots.

"Hi, Pumpkin. What'cha doin'?" Daddy asks.

"Playing cars." I answer.

"Want me to play with you?" He starts toward me.

"No," I say fast. "I'm done." I keep my back to him and my hands between my legs.

"Alright," Daddy says and goes in the house.

Now what? "Come on, go back together," I say out loud to my hands.

I give up. This isn't going to work. I stumble to my feet, run to the door and pound with my foot. Daddy opens it and lets me in. I'm still holding myself together. I get to the washbasin and let go and blood streams out. Dinner's forgotten.

"Dagnabit!" Daddy yells. "What did you go and do?"

Silent tears fall. I can't breathe. I don't dare cry. This is all my fault.

Mama grabs the turpentine.

"Sorry, this is going to hurt bad. We've got to do it to keep infection out," she warns, and pours it in the cut. I bite my tongue to keep from howling. I deserve this hurt. I shouldn't have been playing with a knife

Sharon Holding Three Kittens

*   *   *

Mama's sick. She has to stay in bed. It's okay. I can take care of myself. After all, I'm four and a half I know my way around our farm pretty good. I'll just stay outside so Mama can sleep. I want her to get well fast.

I know, I'll dress the kittens in my doll clothes. It'll be like having live babies. We have three: calico, gray, and a black one. There, Calli and Mouse are all dressed up. I'll just put them in my doll buggy. "Come here, Dina. Dina, come here!" I grab her around the middle and start to put a dress on her. She wiggles, squirms, meows and her eyes are big and scared looking. She bites me and scratches my hand.

"Ouch!" I cry and drop the black ball of fur. "Just for that you don't get to play anymore." When I look in the buggy the other two babies are gone. "I give up."

"What else can I do?" My eyes spy a chain on the backyard lawn where we tied up a goat to mow the grass. "I'll pretend I'm a dog. My owner doesn't want me to run away so he ties me to a chain."

I take the chain and wrap it around my arm but it slips off. Hm. How can I make it so the dog can't run away? I work the chain around and around, in and under, until–yes, the dog can't get away. I pretend to eat, I bark, I howl.

Then I get bored with being a dog. I try to get the chain off, but this dog can't get away. "Oh, dear. What am I going to do?" I howl, I whine, I bark, but no one comes to my rescue. "Help, help me," I cry in my girl voice. No one comes. I sit a long time. I lie down on the cool grass under the Hawthorne tree and fall asleep.

I feel a hand on my shoulder.

"Sharon, Sharon? What's goin' on here?"

It's my grandpa. I tell him, "I was a dog but I got tired of being a dog and wanted out but couldn't get out and…"

He unwinds the chain while I'm talking, and suddenly I'm rescued.

*　　*　　*

It's June and the raspberries are ripe. I love raspberries, especially right off the bush. Daddy's been watering so I better put on my red boots.

Mmm, I say to myself. I can taste them already.

We plant the raspberries on the edge of our farm next to Mrs. McMillan's place. Mrs. M's a nice lady. I play with her Jerry sometimes when he visits. He's the same age as me. He belongs to Mrs. M's daughter.

Look at those big berries hanging there all red and ready to eat. Yum. I stuff them into my mouth as fast as I can pick 'em and move up the outside of the row. Just a few more and I'll quit. Oh, no! I've fallen in a sink-hole. That's what Daddy calls 'em. The water's gone down a gopher hole. Those guys make long tunnels. Oh, no! OH, NO! I'm sinking more.

"HELP! HELP!" I cry as loud as I can. I try to lift out a leg but it won't budge. The other one's stuck too. "Help! I'm stuck!" I yell. I can feel my body sinking more. The mud's up to my knees. "HELP! I'M GOING UNDER. I…NEED… HELP!" I scream.

I hear a door slam. Mrs. McMillan's heard me. Here she comes. "Help!" I call again. She climbs through the fence and stares at me with a grin on her face.

"Looks like you're an old stick in the mud." She laughs. "Give me your hands. I'll pull you out."

I reach for her big hands, she pulls and pulls, and "POP"—out I come, but not my red boots. They're buried in the hole.

"You'll have to dig them out later." She chuckles. "Young lady, you never go walkin' where the water's run all night. Let's get you to the house."

Chapter 14

JUNE, 1946

MY GREATEST RESCUE

Sharon

I'm almost five and old enough to go to my first Vacation Bible School. I can hardly wait. My teacher, Miss Pontius, is home on missionary furlough from South America. I don't know what a missionary does or what furlough means, but I sure like her smile. She tells stories like my mama and changes her voice for the people. I can see them real in my mind. She even acts it out.

On the third day she starts the story with, "How does it feel to be the shortest people in our Bible School? Is it sometimes hard to see around all the tall people?

"When Jesus was living on earth, he walked from town to town and told people about God. In our story today, he's coming into the town where a man named Zacchaeus lived. He was a short, little man and he really wanted to see this man named Jesus. But everyone was so much taller, he couldn't see anything. What could he do? He climbed up a tree, crawled out on a big limb and sat there waiting to see this man everyone was talking about."

I've been a tree-climber all my life. This guy is someone I'd love to play with.

In a whispered secret voice, Miss Pontius said, "There's something else I need to tell you about Zacchaeus. He was a cheat and no one liked him. In fact, no one in town would even speak to him."

Mama always tells me I must tell the truth, be kind and play fair. Maybe this guy wouldn't be good to play with.

"Jesus stopped right under that tree and called to him, 'Zacchaeus, come down.'"

Jesus was good, kind, and loving. Mama says he was perfect. Why would he want to talk to someone like that who's not nice?

My teacher continues, "He scrambled down the tree as fast as he could and stood right in front of Jesus. Jesus said, 'Zacchaeus, I want to go to your house.'

"The little man led Jesus right into his home. When he learned his life wasn't pleasing God, he asked forgiveness. It changed him into a new person. Jesus cleaned up his heart and made him a good man."

Really? Good can happen just like that? My Mama always tells me to be a good girl and please God. Always walk on the path, never walk on someone's lawn, never speak to an adult until they speak to you, always be kind to old people, play what other kids want to play. There's quite a list that good little girls must follow. I forget sometimes. Asking forgiveness is a new idea to me.

Miss Pontius explained, "Jesus wants to forgive you and take away all the bad things in your heart and put himself in there to live with you forever. All you have to do is ask him. If anyone would like to stay after class, I'll pray with you."

I stay. Who wouldn't want Jesus to live with you forever? She prays with me. I feel light. I'm floating. I'm happy. I'm excited.

I float through the other two attic classrooms and down the narrow stairs. I don't remember touching a single step. The other kids are having a puppet show and song time in the sanctuary.

I burst through the small door at the front, throw both arms in the air and shout, "Hey, everybody, Jesus forgave me and he's going to live in me forever!" Everybody cheers and claps.

It's real. It's simple. It's forever.

*　　*　　*

Tom

Susie's teachin' kids in Vacation Bible School at the Community Church. 'Course, she takes Sharon with her. They do stories from the Bible. I know those. Heard 'em when I's a kid. Hoped my girl's too young to get notions 'bout God.

Not so. Taday, she comes home all excited 'bout askin' Jesus ta forgive her. Like a kid that young's done sin. What's I'm s'posed ta do? Now it's two against one, and I ain't 'bout to give in. Had a-nough religion stuffed down my throat. Paw tried to beat it inta me. Didn't work. He beat it outa me. My wall's up and I'm pluggin' my ears. No way they's gonna persuade me. Susie knows how far ta push. How'm I gonna handle my Pumpkin's questions?

Chapter 15

PARENT TIMES

Sharon feeding chickens

Susan

My five-year-old daughter asked Jesus to forgive her sins. It was the happiest day of my life. I cried all day with joy. Does that make sense? I shared the news with Tom when he got home from work. He gave me a "huh." No other reaction or comment. He doesn't understand how important this decision is. He doesn't know Jesus like I do. He blames

God for his father'sbeatings and our lack of children. I pray every day he'll see God differently. Tom's a loving, kind father to Sharon. I know someday he'll get to know our loving, kind, Heavenly Father.

Mornings are Daddy time for our little girl. Tom goes to work at three in the afternoon so morning is work time around our little farm.

Breakfast is ready at 7:00 a.m. It's a hardy meal: pancakes, eggs, and some kind of meat like bacon, ham, or even an occasional steak. It's wonderful to raise our own meat. In winter we have oatmeal too. Oh, and coffee. Always coffee. The only time Tom ever went without coffee was on the Stick Ranch when we were starving. Sharon's a great eater. Gets up just in time for breakfast. At the age of five, she puts away as much as I do.

She loves doing chores with Daddy. They move from gathering eggs and cleaning out the coop, to milking the cow and giving her oats, to feeding the pigs, to gardening, or whatever the seasonal job is. Our little girl works beside Tom, stacking hay with a pitchfork, picking weeds out of radishes, hoeing around the corn and making sure garden ditches aren't plugged up. They make quite a team. After lunch, he sits and reads the comics in the newspaper to her.

After Tom goes to work on swing shift, it's my time with Sharon. We've built with alphabet blocks since she was two. She puts a block, tells me the name of the top letter and the sound it says. We put them together to spell words. The first word was Sharon. Our words are getting complicated. She reads the comics to her daddy. She names the number on the blocks and puts them in order to twenty-six. I think she's ready for school.

At bedtime, my little girl crawls on her daddy's side of the bed, we cuddle, and I tell her stories. My Aunt Bertha loaned books to me when I was her student. I read, read, read. I never forgot those stories.

We don't have money to buy books, so I tell stories: The Three Little Pigs, Little Red Riding Hood, Peter Rabbit, The Princess and the Pea, The Pied Piper, Jack and the Beanstalk…I've told them many times. I let her choose which she wants. Her favorite is Little Red Riding Hood. When I get to the part where the wolf jumps out of the bed dressed in Grandma's clothes, Sharon always says, "Don't tell that part, Mama. Don't say that. Go to the end." We cuddle closer and I quickly go over it to the end. Of course, the story's not complete without, "All the better to eat you with, my dear."

Tom models good hard work. Sharon follows. I try to model patience, learning and living like Jesus. I think Tom and I are turning into good parents. I use Emma's advice every day. "Simple's a good plan. Love, be kind, respect, and encourage; give much, expect much."

Chapter 16

NEIGHBORS

Susan

We spend our afternoon time visiting our neighbors. I want Sharon to know and respect people of all ages. Each one has something to teach her we don't have. Tom's forty, and I'm thirty-five. That seems old, but we're the youngest people in our block. Our neighbors are grandmas and grandpas. Wisdom oozes out of their lives. They've lived through two world wars and the Great Depression. Some have raised kids and some are childless like we were for so long. Sharon and I visit each house at least once a week. They return our love, support us, and aren't afraid to be honest with us. I love these people who welcome our little family any time, day or night. In turn, we try to help them with things they can no longer do.

* * *

Sharon

Mama and I go visiting friends. She says neighbors are family. We visit old people a lot. Old happens when you've been living years and years and your hair gets white or gray.

We sit, talk, and have tea. Sometimes Mama and I do things for them like cleaning, dusting, picking fruit, or washing windows. I think they like us to come.

We go down the road to a white house on the corner to help Mister and Misses Piskulic pick strawberries 'cause they don't have kids to help.

Mama says, "Pick them with the stems on. Be careful not to smoosh them. They sell them for a living."

I watch where I walk, pick only the big red ones, and put them in a Hallock. The Hallock's a little wooden basket. The Hallock goes in a wood flat. When there's twelve in it, Mister takes them to town in his green pickup to sell. He tells me, "I's proud of ye, little girl. You gut verker. Cum verk any time."

Mister has a donkey named Brandy. She's not friendly, but they get along. He says words to her I don't understand. She looks at him, snorts, then pulls the plow. Brandy saves Mister lots of work. Mister digs the whole garden space every spring before he plants lettuce, carrots, radishes, cabbages, turnips, tomatoes, and corn. He sells those too. Sometimes, I give Brandy a treat like an old carrot or apple. I'm careful she doesn't grab my hand with her monster teeth. She chomps it down, gives me a donkey grin and a hee-haw.

Misses comes to our house to visit too. Both Mister and Misses talk funny. Mama says it's 'cause they come from the old country, called Poland. It's a long, long way off. I like to sit beside Misses when she talks.

Her arm's a soft, squishy pillow, and I lay my head on it. When I was two the soft and squishy got the best of me. I was curious. I turned my head and bit her. Not hard. Just enough to see if it felt like biting into Mama's biscuits.

"Vat?" Misses cried. She grabbed my hand and bit my finger. "Der, how dat veel? No gut I tank." I was shocked. Nothing more was said. I never bit another person.

On Easter she gave me a little round plaque with Jesus pulling open his clothes so you see his heart. She reads the words to me, "Sacred heart of Yesus. 'Member he vants you be a gut girl." It's hanging on my wall to remind me.

She brings an egg every year and tells me, "Ez spring and every ting gonta hatch new. Efen our hearts." Misses is a kind lady.

*　*　*

Across from Piskulic's is Mom and Pop Daniel's house. That's where my friend Jerry lives when his dad's rodeo-an; he rides buckin' broncs. Pop keeps cows and horses in his big pasture and sheep when they're having babies. Jerry and I try to ride those fuzzy guys. My short legs can't climb on. I crawl up the fence and jump on the closest one. We get in trouble.

"Those ewes is lambing. Don't you go near them," Pop yells at us. Daddy says his bark's worse than his bite. He also says I could hurt the babies. I won't do it again.

Pop surprises me with two little guys. They're soft, cuddly, and white.

"You've gotta feed 'em cause their mama don't want 'em." Pop calls 'em bummer lambs. I feel sorry for these little babies. What would I do if Mama didn't want me?

Daddy puts nipples on two pop bottles. Each drinks a bottle of milk breakfast, dinner, and supper. They pull hard, and I need all my muscles for this job. It's all I can do to hang onto the bottles. I name them Gertrude and Bucky. I can't turn my back on Bucky. He runs and butts me in the behind. I think he's playing, but I'm gittin' tired of pickin' me off the ground.

Daddy says when it gets cold, I can sell 'em and buy my own coat. I'm trying to do this right. It's too bad Jerry's gone with his dad. It would be easier with two people.

*　　*　　*

Next door to Mom and Pop is Mama's cousin, Lucy, and her husband Everett. He works on the railroad like Daddy. They've got kids older than me—lots of 'em. Ed, Margaret, Clifford, Loretta, and Harvey. Then there's Dale, who's a year younger than me and Patty, who's three years younger. No wonder they've got a big house with an upstairs and downstairs. When we go visit, they play with me. I don't know why they never come to our house. We don't go there much either. Maybe Lucy's too busy with all those kids.

*　　*　　*

"Come, Sharon, we're going to visit Mrs. VanDell." I take Mama's hand and we cross the busy street called Grelle, walk through the alfalfa field to the alley, and visit Mrs. VanDell in her itty-bitty, gray house. It's only got one room.

A little bed is next to the wall. "See those circles on my quilt?" she asks. I nod. "That's a wedding ring pattern. My momma made it. I brought it with me from Holland."

A big, brown dresser is at the bottom of her bed. She keeps her "handiwork" in the bottom drawer. She tries to teach me to do that work, but the string keeps getting tangled up.

I carry wood for Mrs. VanDell and stack it by the door next to the black cookstove. That stove shines like she just polished it. Don't know how she does that. On one end of the stove, there's a round part that looks like a big, black watermelon.

"What's that round thing?" I ask. "We don't have one of those."

"Oh, it's the greatest thing ever, little one." She points to a pipe that goes in back of the stove to the other side. It has a red faucet on its end above her wash pan.

"See, I put water in the reservoir. The fire heats it and when I turn the red handle, hot water comes out. Never turn the red one, Sharon," she warns me. "It gets mighty hot when I've got a fire." I shake my head to let her know I won't.

I know hot water hurts bad. Mama heats water on our cook stove for Saturday night baths. I always get to take the first bath in the big gray tub in front of the stove. Then its Mama's turn, then Daddy's. Mama keeps putting more hot water in after each of us takes a bath. That means there's lots of water in there for Daddy. He's always the dirtiest 'cause he works on the railroad.

One night I was in a hurry to get in. I didn't know Mama hadn't put in the cold water to cool it off yet. I threw one leg into the tub and screamed. Luckily, I only hurt two toes. I won't turn the red faucet.

"Then the blue faucet next to it must be cold," I say, proud that I know there's two kinds of water, hot and cold.

"That's the best cold water in the county. Right from my own well," she says with a smile. "Glad I don't have to pump water no more. It's good your papa piped water in my house. Makes taking a bath easy and I can have tea in no time."

There's a homemade braided rug made of old rags in the middle of her wood floor. She used lots of pretty colors.

"It took three years getting rags from friends to make this rug; six months to braid and sew it. It's special 'cause I can tell you the name of the friend who gave me each piece. It's like always having my friends sitting in the middle of my house."

"I see Mama's blue dress, there. Look, there's my yellow dress I ripped climbing a tree. Part of me's in that rug," I exclaim.

We sit at her table by the window and have tea. She always has cookies she made in the black stove. I don't like the tea much, but I love the cookies she calls sugar babies.

She says, "I make 'em just for you, my sweet little schat baby."

I smell them all the way to my house when she's baking them.

"Can my mama make these?" I ask.

"I give you recipe," she says with a twinkle in her eye. "But I make them for you as long as I can."

Here's what she wrote:

Mix with your hands 1 cup butter and 1/4 cup sugar

Add 1 tablespoon water, 2 teaspoons vanilla and 2 cups of flour. Keep mixing with your hands. It will be sticky. Wet your hands with water and form little balls. Bake until brown then roll in sugar. You can add cinnamon or nutmeg if you want.

Mrs. VanDell's a tiny lady. I'm five years old, and my head comes up to her shoulder. Sometimes I visit her all by myself. I stop and pick a bouquet of the flowers along the fence like I do for Mama in our field.

She tells me stories about coming from Holland with her mister on a boat when she was sixteen; how they traveled days and days in a wagon to get to Idaho. Her mama and daddy died in the old country. Her mister died in the war. She doesn't have kids. She's all alone. It's a good thing she has us.

She tells me, "I'm happy for you to visit, my little schat" (that means "honey").

* * *

Mrs. McMillian lives right by our raspberry patch. Remember, she's the one who rescued me from that sink hole? Her grandson, Jerry, comes to stay with her in the summer. Hey, I've got two Jerry friends, don't I? Mrs. M's Jerry lives in a big town called Spokane. I hope I can go there someday.

He's got red hair and lots of freckles. I'm glad because I've never had a friend with red hair before. We play cars, hide and seek, build things out of boards by his grandma's barn and race around the pasture. The tricky thing in the pasture is not to step in cow pies. The stink never gets out of your shoes.

He has a dog he brings sometimes. I don't like it. When the dog's there, we play at my house. I'm scared of dogs. Daddy brought one home once. We named it Cubby. He jumped on me every time I went outside. He was little, but he jumped hard and knocked me down. I'd climb in a tree where he couldn't reach me and stay there 'till Mama came to rescue me. Jerry's dog does that too. Nope, I won't go there if he brings the dog.

*　　*　　*

Next to Mrs. McMillian's pasture are my favorite neighbors, Grandma and Grandpa Yarber. Grandpa is tall and strong. He's got white hair and a mustache. He lets me help hitch up his horse and wagon. We go up the road and load it with hay for his horse and cow. I know how to use a pitchfork. I help Daddy shock hay all the time. I sit by Grandpa on the wagon, and sometimes he lets me have the reigns and drive the horses.

"Gee, haw." See, I even know their language.

Two times, he's let me go with him all the way to town with their milk cans to sell at the dairy.

"Don't think that's a good idea anymore. Cars are gettin' too thick for a horse and wagon," he said the last trip. He doesn't have a car. Daddy will take his cans to town with ours now.

Grandma's short, round, and pulls her hair tight in what Mama calls a bun. The house always smells like fresh bread or cinnamon rolls. I knock and walk in.

"Sharon, so glad you came to visit us," her happy voice calls from the kitchen. She gives me a hug, a big glass of milk, and one of her famous rolls on the big kitchen table.

"Grandma, you make the best cinnamon rolls. Thank you." I always say thank you. That's the polite thing Mama taught me. I'm not just saying it to be polite. I love those rolls.

I eat and we chatter about what I've been doing since I was here last.

She asks questions. "Do you have your garden planted yet? What did you do this week you've never done before? Did you help Mama this week?" One question is always, "What Bible verse did you learn this week?"

I stand beside my kitchen chair and recite my verse for the week, "For God so loved the world that He gave his only begotten Son that whosoever believes in Him will not perish but have everlasting life. John 3:16." I get a different verse every Sunday in my class, and Grandma makes sure I know it.

"Very good, very good," she says. "You'll always remember that."

When I finish eating, I run to the living room where Grandpa Yarber's reading.

"Sit, sit, sweetheart," he tells me. "I'm reading a book about birds. Look at this beautiful picture of a bluebird. If we took a trip to those mountains we see in the south, we'd see some in person." I sit and he tells me about other birds in the book too. I love birds. They're a happy animal. They like to sing all the time.

Yarbers have a Victrola and lots of records. My favorite songs are "Red Wing" and "Indian Love Call." Grandpa goes to the Victrola, winds it up, winks at me and says, "How about a round of Red Wing."

We sing it out, "Oh, the moon shines tonight on pretty Red Wing ..." We sing so loud you can't hear the scratchy needle going across the record. His old hound dog on the chain outside joins us with howls. We laugh. He gives me a penny for every song, even if I just sing Sunday School songs.

Grandpa's got a funny, long tube with colored glass that moves 'round and makes beautiful looking pictures. He calls it a kaleidoscope. I point it at the kerosene lantern's bright light. "Ooh, ah, pretty." I never get tired of it.

The other thing I love is the stereoscope. He puts two pictures in the frame, and when I look in the other end, I feel like I can walk right into the picture. It's magic, I tell you.

I spend more time at Grandma and Grandpa Yarbers than my real grandma and grandpa 'cause five years old is old enough to walk this far.

Chapter 17

BIG TROUBLE

Sharon's professional picture in taffeta dress

Sharon

It's a hot July. Mama's taking me downtown on the bus to The C. C.
Anderson's Department Store to get my picture taken. I put on my rose
taffeta Christmas dress. It's the prettiest dress I've ever had. I love the
way it makes noise when I move. I got to wear it when Iwas the angel

69

on top of the kid singing Christmas tree at church. No one could see it though, 'cause I had big wings on my back and a long white gown. Other kids were in front of me with tree branches. The whole tree, I mean all the kids, sang lots of songs. I sang "There's a Song in the Air" all by myself.

Now, everyone will get to see my rose dress in my picture. Mama takes a long time to curl my natural curls into dark brown ringlets around her finger. I'm wearing my little heart necklace Grandma and Grandpa Kole gave me for my fifth birthday. I feel like a princess in a fairy tale. I wish we had a mirror so I can see how beautiful I am. I walk carefully. No running or bobbin' up and down. I need to look perfect.

The picture man sits me on a little stool and turns on bright lights that hurt my eyes. I open them wide anyway and smile my very best. The man says I did good, and the pictures will be ready in two weeks. They'll even be in color.

"You did everything just right. I'm proud of you. Shall we go to the donut shop for a treat?" Mama asks.

"Yes, yes, yes. A donut a la mode!" I answer. She smiles and we walk down main street toward the big hotel. "There it is." I'm good at finding places I like.

I smell the donuts cooking before we open the door. The donut shop's not very big. It only has room to walk between the one long counter and a row of booths. We sit at the counter on round red stools. You know, the kind that twirl around.

A lady asks, "What are you having today, Chase family?" See, we've been there often enough she even knows our name.

"Two plain donut a la modes, please," Mama says. Mama always says please. Me too. She pulls out my little apron from her purse and puts it over my head. "Need to protect your beautiful dress from an ice cream spill. It would ruin the taffeta." The lady brings two huge donuts with a big scoop of vanilla ice cream on top. Mmm, one of my favorite things.

The bus ride back home is long. My tummy's full and I'm getting sleepy. Next thing I know, Mama's reaching up to pull the bell cord. That tells the driver we want to get off at the next stop, 20th and Grelle. She takes my hand as we get off.

"Let's go visit Emma and the girls for a bit," she says. Emma is Grandma and Grandpa Yarber's daughter. She lives in the house on the corner. She's got two girls. Janice is older than me, and Shirley is younger. They're my friends. We like each other a lot. Mama and Emma visit; we play with dolls a while, then go outside.

A long path goes between Emma's house and the Yarber's. The garden up by the street's been watered. It came downhill making perfect mud in the path. "Look at this!" I exclaim, pulling off my black patent shoes and white socks. "Ooey, gooey, slimy mud. Let's go wading."

Janice looks at me with scared eyes. "Is that a good idea? You're dressed up."

"I'll be careful. I'm just going to get my feet muddy." I step into the cool mud. "Mud, mud, wonderful mud." They take off their shoes and follow me.

We get a little rambunctious, as Mama would say, and start running and sliding. It's my third slide when my feet lose control and *splat*—down I go.

"Ooh, it feels so cool and slimy. Did I say I love mud? It's squishy stuff." Making mud pies is my favorite. "Come on, let's go mud swimming." I yell and we all roll in the ooey, gooey. I didn't plan on falling, but I'm here so might as well enjoy.

"Sharon Aleen Chase!" Mama yells. "What in the world are you doing?"

"Pl...play...in' in the mud," I answer, not sure what's going to happen. Mama's only used that tone of voice once before in my whole life. At three, I drew a rocking horse on the bedroom wall with my new crayons. She was so mad, she spanked me with the hairbrush. It's the only time I've been spanked. Strange she's never washed it off or covered it up. Guess she left it there to remind me what naughty is.

"Crack!" I look up quick. Mama broke a limb off the willow tree. "Your dress, Sharon. Look at your dress. It's ruined. What were you thinking?" Jumping up, I look down at my dress. It's not rose. Thick globs of mud are dripping off. I try to clean it with my hands. They're full of mud, too. Big trouble!

Mama picks up my socks and shoes, grabs me by the arm and begins whipping my legs. Willow branches sting. I don't dare say a word. We march down the road toward home. She doesn't talk 'til we get to our back door.

"Strip," she orders. "Wash every bit of that mud off with the hose before you come in the house."

I follow directions. The water's cold. It takes a long time to get rid of the mud— especially out of my hair. I'm embarrassed standing in our backyard bare-naked.

She throws me an old towel and a cotton dress to put on. There are tears in her eyes. She still doesn't speak. I tiptoe in the house and crawl in my bed. Mama's mad at me. What I did was wrong. Yup. Big trouble!

*   *   *

Susan

I'm a failure. An utter failure. All of Emma's wisdom and advice flies right out of my mind when I see what my daughter's doing. Her dress—her beautiful, expensive, pink taffeta dress! It's ruined, totally ruined. I'm angry. I go right to the place my mama would have been, break off a willow switch and swat her legs all the way home. I demand she cleans herself up in the backyard and I go in the house and fall apart.

"Oh, God. What did I just do? I switched my little girl. Now she's going to think I don't lover her. What was I thinking? I'm a rotten mother. How am I ever going to tell Tom?" I cry as I pour out my horrible deed to God.

"Mama, I'm clean." Sharon calls. I throw her a towel and an everyday dress and quickly close the screen. I don't want her to see me crying. My heart is broken, and I must ask forgiveness.

Chapter 18

THE RESERVATION

Susan

Jimmy, Papa's youngest brother, married Tom's sister, Grace. Tom was working harvest on their farm near Reubens when I met him. I think there was some conniving between my mother and Grace to get us married. We took it seriously and had a wedding three months after we were introduced.

In '43, they started a mission on the Nez Perce Indian reservation. The tribe hunts, fishes, and digs native plants. Income is scarce. Food runs out in the winter. Families are poor.

Tom and I have a special relationship with these people. One of their hunters saved us from starvation our first winter on the Stick Ranch. We call him Friend. These are good people.

*   *   *

Sharon

We go over the hill and down a windy, dirt road to the reservation to visit Aunt Grace and Uncle Jim. Their house is always full of people coming and going, eating, making quilts, canning, talking, sorting clothes, kids running everywhere. Mama and Daddy help. I get to play with these kids. Their games are different than at the Snyder's. They use sticks instead of cans, and they sing a lot during the games. I don't know the words. They teach me.

Grandma Jackson practically lives at Uncle Jim's house. She loves Jesus a whole bunch and comes to help. Grandmas out there, take care of the kids. Paul's always there with her. He's my age. He teaches me games, words, and how to make something called weaving.

"Just look at that little girl out there playing with all those little Injun kids," Grandma Jackson said to my mama one day as she watched us out the window. "You don't see that often enough." When mama told me that, I thought it was strange. I love being here. How come more people don't come visit?

Oh, man! Can Grandma Jackson sing. She sits, third bench back, behind the piano Aunt Grace plays for church. You can hear her high voice singing all over Lapwai. She always asks to sing, "When the Roll is Called Up Yonder." We sing in English. She belts it out in Nez Perce:

Wewanekitpa himuna, wewanekitpa himunu,
wewanekitpa himunu.

Ka kunah nakai in witastatasham.Yup.

These are special people. I love 'em and they love me.

Chapter 19

VISITS TO TOWN

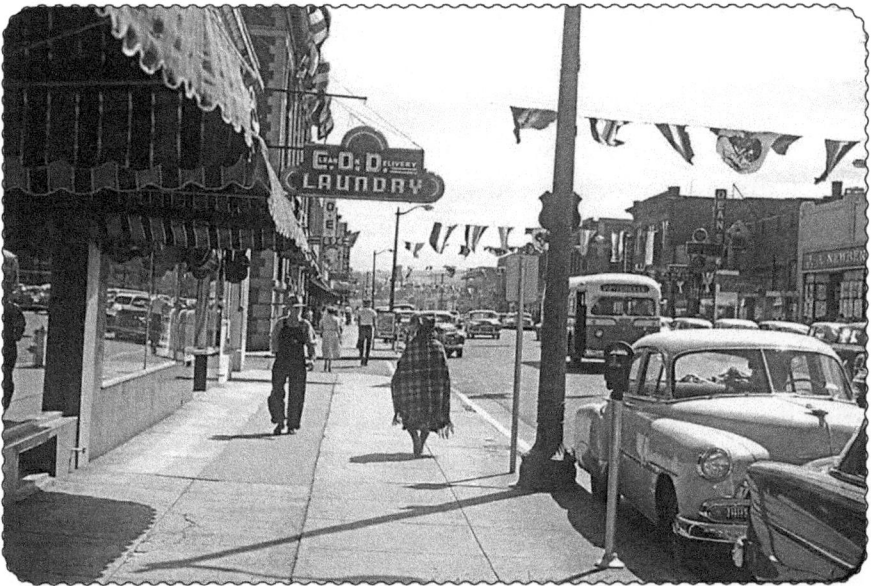

Lewiston's Main street

Sharon

"It's town day, it's town day." I sing as I skip through the house.

"Yes, it is," responds Mama. "That day also has another name, Saturday. We go to town on Saturday."

"Saturday?" I ask.

"All the days have names. I know a song that'll help you remember them." She starts singing.

> "This is the way we go to town
> Go to town, go to town.
> This is the way we go to town
> all on a Saturday morning."

I sing along as we get ready.

We dress up for town day, oops, I forgot—Saturday, but not in our church clothes. I scrub my face and hands, comb my hair and brush my teeth. I'm learning to brush my teeth. I shake the powder stuff called Colgate in my hand, get my red toothbrush wet and rub it in the powder. I make a funny face and pull back my lips and wash my teeth. I brush hard and fast. Yuck, the powder tastes awful. I spit and spit and spit. Mama lets me rinse it out with water. Thank goodness I only have to brush when we're going someplace.

I run out to the car and climb in the front seat. Daddy always drives and Mama sits by the other window. I'm like a kid sandwich. The problem is, I can't see much. When I was little, I sat on Mama's lap. Now I'm too big. So, I have to look at the trees and telephone poles. I don't like some things about being five.

"We're picking up Grandma and Grandpa to take them to town with us. It helps them save gas stamps," Mama says. "They'll need the gas rations to take their berries to town in June." Grandma and Grandpa are old. Both of them have lots and lots of wrinkles on their faces.

Grandpa doesn't have much hair on top of his head, but he has big, hairy eyebrows. Grandma has white hair. Her eyes aren't like the rest of us. They're the color of the robin's egg I found in the yard last summer. Grandpa, Mama and I have brown eyes and Daddy's are kind of yellow and brown, but Grandma's are blue. She always wears earrings the same color as her eyes. I love looking at her eyes.

It's not far from their house to town.

"Where da you need to go, Papa?" Daddy asks.

"I wanna get wire and a new handle for my hammer, so probably Montgomery Ward's or Sears," Grandpa answers. "Could you park on main street so Mama can sit in the car and watch people if she gets tired?"

"Hey, look!" I yell. "There's a place right in front of Monkey Wards." I'm always good at finding parking places when I can scootch up on Mama's lap. Daddy parks and we all pile out. We don't even get in the store before Daddy stops to talk to Mr. Gunter, who lives up our street at the top of the hill. Town Day means visiting, visiting, visiting. Mama and Daddy know everyone.

"Monkey Wards" is an exciting place. It has high, high ceilings and stairs that go up to women's clothes, then up to furniture. We don't go to furniture much. We already have that stuff. Stairs go down too, all the way down underground. That's where they sell things like Grandpa's hammer and wire. Best of all, way back in the corner of the underground, are toys.

When I was little Daddy would call, "Up you go, Pumpkin." His strong arms grabbed me around the middle and swung me up to sit on his shoulders. I could see the whole store from up there.

"Watch your head and duck," he'd warn me. I never bumped my head.

When I was three, Daddy took me to the basement to see Santa before Christmas. I knew he wasn't a real guy 'cause Mama told me it's just a game we play. I like that game so I sat on his knee and told him, "I'd like a dolly with brown eyes like me, please."

Santa said, "Look at me. I want to see those brown eyes."

"See," I looked him straight in the eyes. "Oh," I squealed, "You've got brown eyes too."

He laughed and gave me a candy cane and a book, "Rudolph the Red-Nosed Reindeer." My very own book! Mama read and read and read it to me. She still reads it to me every Christmas.

After I talked to Santa, Mama took me to the toy department. There were lots and lots, 'cause Christmas was coming and that way kids got ideas what to ask Santa for. We got to the doll part and sitting right in front of my eyes was … guess what? Yup. A brown-eyed doll. "Look, Mama, a brown-eyed doll." I was excited. I knew not to ask to buy it 'cause I'd already ask Santa for one. I didn't need two. Christmas came and Santa remembered. My brown-eyed doll looked just like the one on the shelf.

I'm too big to ride on Daddy's shoulders anymore. I get to explore the store while the big people get what they need. Mama says, "It's okay, but you have to stay in the toy department until we come get you." I always obey. Mama knows what's good for me. Besides, Jesus told me to obey my parents.

When we leave Monkey Wards, we go across to Newberry's. This is my second-best store. They have a whole row of glass boxes full of candy. I get to pick one kind and get a penny's worth. Today I get chicken bones. They're hard, but make little flakes in my mouth. They taste like butter and coconut. My other ones I like are marshmallow peanuts and Boston baked beans. Daddy always gets old fashioned chocolates. He keeps them in the icebox, but I'm not allowed to have them.

In the middle of Newberry's is a big deep box in the toy aisle. It's full of little sacks. You pay a nickel for a sack. You can't open it 'til after you buy it. They call it a grab bag. I've got a nickel Grandpa Yarber gave me for singing. I lift and shake each bag, trying to guess what's in them. I choose the one that's the heaviest and it rattles. Mama gets new oilcloth for our kitchen table, Daddy buys some shoe polish, and I pay for my grab bag. Mama says, "Don't open it until we get in the car. You don't want to lose anything." I know she's right, so I just carry it.

We go to the grocery store last. Segman's Market has squeaky floors, strange smells, and a shiny round bar like a fence where you go pay. I swing and climb on that bar while Mama and Daddy pay and count out their ration stamps. I think they put it there so kids like me have something to do so big people can think.

Mama and Daddy buy a bag of sugar, coffee, and a box of white stuff they call oleo. We use it like butter when our cow quits giving milk 'cause she's gonna have a baby. It's my job to make this white stuff look like butter. It's got a little pack with a yellow pill inside. Mama cuts it in small pieces and puts it on the white glob. I mix it with my hands until it's not white anymore. It looks like butter, but it doesn't taste like butter. My hands look like butter, too—for a long time.

Grandpa joins us and picks up salt and a sack of flour with little roses all over it. I wonder if Grandma will make me a dress from that sack? Grandma's sitting in the car watching all the people go by. She loves to do that.

After he pays, Grandpa says, "How 'bout I treat you to lunch?"

"Oh, boy," I squeal and start climbing on one of the green stools at the long counter by the front door. I'm still not tall enough to get on by myself. Will I ever be big enough?

"Here Pumpkin," Daddy says, "I'll help you up." It's easy when you've got someone as big as Daddy helping. "What'll ya have?" he asks me.

"I already know. I want a fried bologna sandwich. I love that kind." Bologna's special 'cause we never get that at home. We have meat that comes from pigs, calves and chickens, but it's not like bologna.

I feel like a big girl sitting on that stool. I can see people all over the store. I twirl around on my high seat with a back while I wait. The lady behind the counter puts a plate in front of me with my sandwich cut in two pieces and a big slice of pickle. I eat all that yummy stuff slow, to make it last. I finish and Daddy ruffles my hair. "Time to head home, Pumpkin." Can you tell what Daddy's name is for me?

Grandpa buys a donut for Grandma, and we all climb in the car. I'm tired. So tired I fall asleep on Mama's arm and don't wake up 'til we get home. I didn't even hear when we let Grandma and Grandpa off at their house.

Town day—I mean Saturday, is exciting but I'm glad it's only one day of the week. What was in my grab bag? Marbles, bright, shiny, glass marbles.

Daddy's going to teach me how to play.

Grandma and Grandpa Kole

*   *   *

We visit Grandma and Grandpa at least once a week. They live in the other end of the Orchards. Their house used to be the water district office. It's got a beautiful window picture in the door. Someone carved an elk in the glass. I love, love, love, that picture.

Grandpa made the front part into a living room and dining room and the back part into a kitchen and bedroom. There's a barn, the outhouse, and a chicken coop out back. The rest of the place is a raspberry patch, a blackcap patch, walnut trees, and fruit trees.

There's lots of pickin' to do, and there's only two of them. When it's pickin' season, Mama and I go on the bus every day to help. My cousin, Patty, helps too. She's three years older than me. She picks fast. Grandpa gives us a penny for every Hallock of berries we pick.

He doesn't let us kids pick the fruit. In fall, we pick up the walnuts when they're on the ground, peel off the skin and put them in boxes. My hands turn all brown. Grandpa puts them behind the wood heater to dry. I like to stir them. You have to do that every day. Right before Christmas, Patty and I get the job of cracking them and putting them in bags for Grandpa to sell. We're useful kids to have around.

Chapter 20

1945

SCHOOL, OR NOT TO SCHOOL

the Lewiston Orchards School in 1931

Orchard's school

Susan

"And that's the end," Sharon says when she finishes reading her Little Golden Book, "The Animals of Farmer Jones."

"And the pigs were much too busy eating." She laughs.

Our little girl's learning fast. Her daddy reads comics in the Lewiston Morning Tribune to her every day. When Mrs. Pisculik, our

Polish neighbor, comes she reads them out loud too. She says it gives her a reason to learn English better. I read a Bible story to Sharon every day, and now she's reading herself. I know she's ready for school, There's a birthday cut-off date of October 1. Sharon won't be six until November 7.

It's August. I call my friend Edith, whose daughter, Judy, won't be six until the end of October.

"Maybe we could get our girls together to do some learning. It's a shame to waste a whole year without schooling."

"Let me see what I can find out first," Edith answers. "I know Miss McSorley. I'll talk to her tomorrow."

Two days later, my phone rings. It's Principal McSorley.

"Mrs. Chase? I understand you have a girl who's ready for school. I talked to Edith yesterday about Judy starting and decided both Judy and Sharon should start first grade next month."

"Oh, my," I exclaim. "That's wonderful. When's school start?"

"September 10, eight o'clock. I need you to come by and fill out some papers this week. She'll be in Miss Warren's class. I'm looking forward to having Sharon in our school."

"Thank you, thank you very much. You've relieved a huge worry. We'll be there on Wednesday. That's my husband's day off." I hang up the phone and hurry to find Sharon.

She's in the corn field putting oil in the tassels to keep worms out of the ears. "Sharon, Sharon," I call as I run to her. She drops her oil can and sprints toward me.

"What? What's wrong?" she cries.

"You're going to start school on September 10th." She squeals and jumps on me, almost knocking me down. "I just talked to Miss McSorley, the principal. She's going to let both you and Judy start school this year." We hug each other tight and hop up and down with joy.

*   *   *

Tom, Sharon, and I are on our way. I won't believe it's true until we get the enrollment done.

"There it is, there it is!" Sharon shouts. We've driven by The Orchards School on the corner of Thain and Burrell many times. It's a two story, stone building built in 1912. It looks more like a hospital. We walk in the doublewide, window-paned, front doors and down five steps into a huge open hall. The dark wooden floor creaks as we walk. I imagine it filled with noisy children. A pungent odor comes from a large cheese-looking block on a table outside the principal's office in the far-left corner. I wonder what that is. Tom and I are nervous and excited. Sharon is just excited.

"Mr. and Mrs. Chase and Sharon, welcome to The Orchards School." Miss McSorley greets us. She's a short, chunky lady with frizzy red hair pulled to the back in a bun. Her smile is almost as wide as her entire face. She wears gold, wire-rimmed glasses that make her blue eyes look big and wise. Yes, I would say she has an owl face except for the smile. She immediately makes us feel comfortable.

"Here's the information I need you to fill out." She takes our daughter's hand. "Sharon, while Mom and Dad are working on that, I'll take you to see your classroom. It just so happens your teacher's here today getting ready for you students. You'll get to meet her." They walk across the wide hall to the first door. I can hear my daughter chattering excitedly.

By the time Miss McSorley and Sharon return, we've finished the registration. Sharon's glowing.

"Guess who my teacher is?" she shouts. "Miss Warren from next door to Aunt Neen. She taught my Sunday School class last year. I already know my teacher."

"Nice lady, Miss Warren. I like her mother and father too. You're gonna love school. We'd better buy you a pencil and some crayons. Maybe even a new dress," Tom says with a smile.

He's proud of his little girl and gives her a big hug. I see sadness in his eyes. His little girl- buddy's growing up. They've been constant companions when he's not at work. He's put in at the railroad for a change from swing shift to night shift, so he'll be awake when she gets home from school.

We'll practice being quiet so he can sleep, especially in winter. The newspaper insulation in our walls isn't soundproof. Maybe we can put the real stuff in this fall. It would help with warmth too. Frost forms inside the windowpanes thick enough to write your name when cold attacks outside. Thank goodness our wood stoves keep us toasty warm.

* * *

Change is coming. The Inner Voice speaks, "Sharon's watched your example, walked your bridge, and become My child. She's putting stones in her own structure, beyond yours into the future. You'll remain a strong, secure support whenever her bridge falls apart. Listen, watch, and speak wisely. I'll never leave you. Trust me."

First Day of 1st Grade Sharon

* * *

Sharon

Big surprise! Miss McSorley, the principal, calls Mama and says, "Judy's mother has persuaded me to let her into first grade so Sharon might as well come too."

"Yippee! I get to go to school."

The bad thing is, I have to get a shot. Mama takes me to Doctor Carsow. He tells me to lift up my dress. What? My mama tells me good girls never to do that. I shoot a quick look at her. She nods. I'm embarrassed and shocked, but I follow orders. Ouch! Boy, did that shot hurt.

On the first day, Daddy and Mama drive me to school.

"How do I look? Where do I go when we get there? Will I know anybody? I forgot to ask where the toilet is. Oh, look at all the kids standing in line. How do I know what line to get in? I see, I see. There's Miss Warren. I'll be in her line, won't I?" I chatter away. When the car stops, I hop out.

"Wait for us," Mama calls. "We want to go with you on the first day."

"Hurry, hurry," I plead. "I don't want to be last in line." I pull Mama's hand so she'll go faster. I put myself in Miss Warren's line and look up at Mama and Daddy.

"Yup. This is where I belong." There're tears in their eyes. Are they happy or sad?

I stand in front of The Orchards School with my new pencils, crayons, and a lunch box. My new red dress and finger curled brown ringlets are perfect. I'm waiting, waiting, waiting. Miss McSorley comes out the door and blows a whistle. Everyone hushes.

"Hand over your heart, eyes on the flag. 'I pledge allegiance ...'" Miss McSorley begins.

Oh dear, I don't know those words. We sing "America." A teacher reads from the Bible, "This is the day the Lord has made. Let us rejoice and be glad in it." We say the Lord's Prayer. I know that from Sunday School. Finally, we go two by two following our teacher.

Miss Warren takes us right into our room.

"Look for your name on a table," her quiet voice instructs. "When you find it, sit down."

Gordon, a neighbor friend, is crying in the corner. I take his hand and lead him back to sit by me. My teacher puts an extra chair by mine.

"You can sit by Sharon today." She nods and points to the chair and begins to sing. "I'm glad you are here, I'm glad you are here, I'm glad you came to school today, I'm glad you are here."

I'm glad too.

*   *   *

Miss Warren went to Italy last summer. She's excited about her trip and tells all about that country. We tear up newspaper, mix it with flour and water and build a map of Italy on a board as big as the table. There're mountains and lakes. It looks like a giant boot. When it gets dry, we paint it. Miss Warren cooks spaghetti for us. Those long strings are a first for me. Mmm. It's yummy.

My best time is when Miss Warren reads to us. I want to read like she does. She makes up voices. She gets excited when Peter Rabbit's being chased. I hold my breath, hoping he doesn't get caught. I'm sorry when he has a tummy ache. I know how he feels. At the end of the book, we celebrate Peter's escape by drinking chamomile tea with lots of milk and sprinkles of nutmeg. Never had that before, either.

Another first is a band. Miss Warren calls it a rhythm band. "Tap, tap, tap tap-tap," I play my drum I got for last Christmas. My beat must be good 'cause she chooses me to be the "student director" for "The March of the Wooden Soldiers."

We play at the Grange Hall, flower clubs, women's clubs and churches. That little tin drum of mine gets a special place every morning in front of the school at "opening ceremonies" for the rest of the year. I beat out a rhythm while all the kids march in.

There are lots of firsts. Is that why they call it first grade?

*   *   *

I take a bucket and go looking for rocks. Twenty. I need twenty, I say to myself. That's how far I was told we have to count in first grade. I find sticks too. They're easy 'cause we have trees galore on our place. Peach trees, pear trees, prune trees, apple trees and shade trees. Mama says shade trees help keep our house cool in summer. I set up my school in the front yard under the biggest shade trees. I'm gonna be the teacher and have neighbor kids in my class.

I write a note to each family and invite them to come to my school. Surprise! Five little kids come. Three of them are Snyders. They've

86

added Marilyn and Glenna. That makes eleven kids at their house, four boys and seven girls. Four plus seven makes eleven. Yeah! I can add pretty high.

I tell the story of Jack and the Bean Stalk; we count to twenty using rocks and sticks, and then we play a game of tag for recess. Tomorrow, we'll do addition. I know lots of things to teach them.

The second week of my school, Grandpa Kole brings me a board painted black with a brown frame and three pieces of chalk. Now it's a real school. This is gonna' be a great summer.

Chapter 21

LESSONS, CARNIVAL, AND PUPPIES

Sharon First day of 2nd Grade

Sharon

Moving to second grade's easy. In Mrs. Lambert's class, there're workbooks. I love workbooks. I work page after page and read, read, read in our reading book. I finish three before the end of September. I tackle math pages with a passion. It's a game. Can I do the next page? I give it a try. Mrs. Lambert sits me close to the front where she can keep an eye on me.

"Sharon," she scowls at me, "You cannot work ahead. You haven't had the lesson yet. I'll take away your workbooks if you don't quit."

I try. What am I supposed to do when I'm done and the other kids aren't? I look in my desk and find my big yellow notebook Daddy bought for school. Aha, here's the answer. I write stories about my adventures: getting stuck in a gopher hole, chained like a dog, falling into the pigpen.

Judy's in my class too. We're best friends. That's 'cause we're the littlest in the class. We play together at recess. Our favorite thing is teeter totter. Up and down, up and down, up and down. I see other kids doing bumps on the ground trying to get the kid on the other end off.

Hm, I wonder if I can bounce Judy off. The next time I'm down, I push really hard. The board hits the ground. "Thud." Judy falls off and lands on her face. She comes up screaming and crying with blood running down her chin and a tooth in her hand. She runs into the school. I feel awful. I hurt my best friend.

Even though I said sorry, Judy doesn't play with me anymore.

*   *   *

Carnival Night

They set up tables for people to play Bingo, a fishing pond, a dart contest to pop balloons, and a food table in the big hall on the first floor. I can't wait. The fishing pond's my favorite. You never know what you'll catch: a piece of candy, a balloon, a windmill, a cookie.

"Are you ready, Sharon," Mama calls.

"Yup! Ready steady," I answer. I've discovered rhyming and try to rhyme everything I say. I giggle. Sometimes I have to make up words so they'll rhyme.

We jump in the car. Daddy always drives, I'm in the middle and Mama by the window. The whole school's lit up. We stop at a table by the door. Daddy buys tickets. He hands me ten so I can go do what I want. Mama and Daddy mostly eat, visit, and play Bingo. I try that game too. It's okay, but one game's enough.

I head for the fishing pond. On the way, I peak in the third-grade room. What's that? I walk in. A man closes the door behind me and puts a finger to his lips in a "Shhh." I watch. A big girl's talking into a long, black, stick thing. She's saying a poem, I think.

She's done. A man shuts off a machine and says, "Next?"

"What's this?" I ask the man.

"It's a recorder," he explains. "You talk or sing in here and this machine puts it on a record."

"How many tickets?" I want to know.

"One for each side. Would you like to try?" He inquires.

"Yes, yes. Can I sing two songs?"

"Oh course, but you have to stop in between so I can turn the record over." He holds up a small pink circle.

"Oh, goodie. It'll be a surprise for Mama and Daddy."

I belt out, "I Will Sing the Wondrous Story," a song I learned at church. He turns it over and I sing "There's a Song in the Air." That's the song I sang when I was on the top of the Christmas tree. The room's very quiet when I'm done.

"That was beautiful," the man whispers. "What's your name?"

"Sharon Chase," I whisper back and giggle.

"Come back in half an hour and we'll have your record ready." He winks and I skip out the door. I made a record. I get to hear my own voice.

After playing lots of games, my tickets are gone, and I sneak into the record room. There it is; a little pink record in a bag with my name on it. I hold it carefully.

When we get home, I play it for Mama and Daddy on our wind-up phonograph. It makes their eyes sparkle.

Record that Sharon recorded

*   *   *

Sometimes Mama and I go to Richardson's house on 20th street to help her pick raspberries. She's got a grandson named Jerry. My goodness, that makes three Jerrys I know. It must be a popular name.

This morning Mrs. Richardson calls and talks to Mama a long time. I come in from playing as Mama's saying, "I'll talk to Tom about it and let you know."

It's summer vacation. I spend mornings exploring on my own. After Daddy comes home around three-thirty, I hear them talking in quiet, secret voices in the bedroom.

"Sharon," Mama calls. I find them both sitting on the bed. "Mrs. Richardson needs something done. She asks if you can come help. Would you like to do that?"

"Sure," I respond. "Now?"

"It's a good time, but you have to go alone. It's time for me to start dinner."

"I can do that," I say as I start out the door. "How long can I stay?"

"Come back when she tells you." Daddy answers.

The long walk gives me time to think about what she wants me to do—pick tomatoes, shell peas, snap beans ... can't be raspberries, I picked those last month. She answers my knock with a big smile on her face.

"Come in, come in." she holds the screen door open. "I have something very important for you to do."

She leads me to the end of the long, screened porch and takes down a short wood fence. There's her dog, Jelly, in a big box with five little puppies. I made friends with the mama dog when I picked raspberries. She's different from Cubby, who bit at me and trapped me in the front yard tree when I was four years old.

I kneel down and pet Jelly's head. Her kind, brown eyes and the way she licks my hand, says she likes me.

Mrs. Richardson kneels beside me. "Sharon, I need your help with the puppies. They're old enough to be on their own. I want you to pick out one to take home."

"Me?" I question. "You want to give me one of them?"

"Yes. I know you'll be kind and take good care of it. Which one do you want?"

"Oh, dear. Can I hold them? This is a hard decision." She nods and goes in the house, leaving me to get acquainted.

When she returns, I'm holding my pick of the litter. She's black with a white ring around her neck and down her chest. Her kind, brown eyes are just like her mama's.

"Look how she cuddles in my arms and goes to sleep. This is the one I want. Is it okay with Mama and Daddy?"

She nods, wraps my little girl in a piece of old blanket, and I walk my prize home. By the time I reach my house, I have a name for her; Lassie—like the hero dog on the radio program.

Chapter 22

A BIGGER WORLD

Susan

This trip to Portland will certainly enlarge our world. I've never traveled farther than one hundred miles from Lewiston. I'm nervous, fearful for my family. I know Tom's been there before visiting his sister when his mother was alive, but so many things can happen.

It's important we go. I want Sharon to have a bigger world view than I live in. I'll remember God's on the train; He's in Portland, He's at the ocean, and wherever we go. I trust Him to take care of us.

*   *   *

My First trip

Sharon

Remember my friends, Shirley and Janice, where I played in the mud between their house and their Grandma and Grandpa's? I find out Shirley puts ants in a bowl with sugar and cream and eats them. Yuck! I watch her do that. They're still alive. Something's wrong with that girl. I also found out they're moving away this summer. That makes me sad.

I don't have time to think much about this 'cause Mama, Daddy and I are going on a long train ride to Portland to visit my Aunt Frankie and Uncle Walt. They have three kids: Nyella, Mary Jane, and David.

Daddy takes me to the railroad yard where he works sometimes. I climb up in the engine cab, ring the bell and look into the big fire box that makes the steam to run the train. This will be the first time I get to ride in one of those cars it pulls.

"Come on, Sharon," Mama calls. "We're going to Montgomery Ward's to get a suitcase. What color shall we get?"

"Blue," Daddy and I say at the same time. We laugh and head to town.

The minute we walk up the stairs to the suitcases, we spot it—blue, with a gold handle and made out of cardboard. All our clothes will go in there.

I can't get to sleep tonight. I'm seven years old. I've been to Grangeville, Stites, Reubens, Orofino, and of course Clarkston. I know about Lewiston. That's where I live. It's a big city, but Daddy says Portland's a big, big city. How long will this take? What will I see? Will I get lost? This is an adventure like I listen to on the radio.

"Sharon, it's time to get ready. Aunt Neen will be here to take us to the depot soon." Mama gently wakes me.

I hop out of bed and pull on my brown, bibbed pants and checked blouse. Mama thinks pants are better than a dress for this trip. I wolf down my oatmeal, Mama combs my hair into ringlets, and we stand in the driveway waiting for Aunt Neen.

Lots of people are waiting to get on the train. Daddy has our passes ready. We ride the train for free because he works on the railroad. Our pass says, "car three and seats three and four". That's easy to find. They face each other. That's good. We can talk better and share our lunches we brought.

The engine's stoked and ready to go. It's noisy. Thick smoke comes out the chimney. It's a good thing the wind's blowing or we couldn't see the train. "Chug, chug, chug, squeak, slam, whoo, whoo." The train makes all kinds of sounds as we creep away from the depot.

"Yeeeaaah!" I squeal and clap my hands. Mama and Daddy smile. I've never been this excited in my whole entire life.

The train's goes faster and faster. I see hills, brush, trees; then there's nothing but sand and some bushes.

Daddy says, "'Member them big brown clouds rollin' t'ward Lewiston and I say 'Pasco dust storm's comin'? This here's that dirt. Wind picks it up here and dumps it on us."

I remember all right. It's brown fog so thick you can't see anything or breathe. You don't go outside. The brown stuff comes through cracks around windows and walls. I have to dust for days to get it off the furniture (that's my job in the house—dusting). All I see is sand, dirt and little bushes Mama calls sage brush. This is boring.

I fall asleep.

I wake up when the train stops.

"Oh, good. You're awake," Daddy says. "We git an hour to stay here and see the falls." "What falls?" I ask. The only falls I've seen are in the spring when the snow's melting and water runs down the rocks on the hills.

"It's called Celilo Falls. Boats cain't go up it. People half ta carry everything from one boat 'round the falls ta another boat up the river a piece. Indians got a stand over it. They go out there with a net and catch fish jumpin' up the falls. Let's go watch."

As soon as we go 'round the big rocks, I can't breathe. Never, ever have I seen so much water. It's pouring over monstrous rocks. It's nothing but white foam by the time it gets to the rest of the river below. It goes all the way 'cross the whole river. It's twice as wide as our Lewiston river. I stare. It's beautiful, but it scares me. I don't want to go too close. I'm afraid it'll reach up and grab me.

"See that man out there on the stand fishin'?" Daddy points. I see alright. My heart almost stops. I feel dizzy like when I hit my head. The man's got a long pole with a net on the end. He's leaning on the railing at the end of the stand. A fish jumps up the white foam toward the top of the water. The man leans out even more. He's quick. He grabs the fish in the net. People around us clap and cheer. The man turns around and smiles at us.

"Oh, that's scary," I say with a shaky voice. "What happens if the water grabs him?"

"I'm thinkin' the rail's strong," Daddy assures me. We watch 'til the train whistles for us to climb on board. I've got a picture of Celilo Falls plastered in my brain I'll never forget.

Fishing at Celilo Falls

Outside there're changes—mountains, lots of trees, and big rocks with no trees. It's green, green, green, and the river is blue, blue, blue.

The train slows but doesn't stop. The conductor announces, "Look left and you'll see Multnomah Falls." I suck in my breath.

Another waterfall? Ooh, a tall, tall one with a little bridge across it. It's beautiful, but not scary. It might be if I was on the bridge.

"Only two more hours to Portland," he adds.

*   *   *

Uncle Walt's waiting for us at the Portland depot. It's a big place and there are lots of tracks and trains. We follow him outside to the car. I stay close and hang onto Mama's hand.

"Oh . . . Oh . . . look how tall." I stop walking so I can look to the top of the building across the street. My head is all the way back.

"How can they build something that big? Do people live up there? How do they get there?" Everyone chuckles.

"We'll go in one later," Daddy says. He's been to Portland before, so he knows all about this place.

97

The drive to my aunt's house is long, but I can't stop looking. I mustn't blink. I'll miss something.

"There's an airplane on top of the gas station," I yell.

"Yep, it's called Bomber Gas," Uncle Walt explains. "We're gonna stop and get gas there." He drives under the big wing and waits for the gas guy to fill up the car. "See those trees over there," he points. "We call them monkey tail trees. They belong to the fir family. You don't wanna touch their needles. They're hard and sharp. Sorta pretty though."

We get to their house, and everyone pours out of the house to give hugs. Nyella's old, sixteen, I think. MaryJane is thirteen, and David is three years younger than me. I find out right away David's spoiled. He gets his own way about everything. We go to bed early 'cause we're tired. We're getting up early to go see the ocean. David refuses to go to bed. He kicks and screams his head off when his mother tries to take him to bed. Mama calls that a temper tantrum.

*   *   *

"The ocean, the ocean, we're gonna see the ocean," I sing as I run around the living room after breakfast. There's a bag packed with food, a stack of towels, and we're each taking an extra set of clothes—just in case. "Seaside, seaside ..." I sing as I bounce out to the car. There's eight of us plus our stuff, so I sit on Mama's lap and David sits on Nyella's. "Three in the front and three in the back and two on top," I continue to sing as we head west.

The hum of the car and people talking makes me sleepy. I won't close my eyes. I don't want to miss a single thing. Hills, cars, little towns, trees, windy roads, Oh, dear, I hope no one gets car sick.

We come around a long curve and Aunt Frankie calls, "There it is. There's the ocean. My, ain't it purty?"

I can't tell you how I'm feeling. Ocean-whelmed, maybe. I've never seen so much water. This is even scarier than the falls. It never ends. I'm suddenly quiet.

Turn around at Seaside

We go to the aquarium. It's got all kinds of things that live in that big water: crabs, lobsters, fish, sharks, eels . . . even a little octopus. That makes the ocean even more frightening.

We hear a woman screaming, "Help! I need help!" A loud horn bellows across the beach just outside the front door. People start running from every direction Some head for the water. Some run out of the water. Some carry two poles. Some have a big tank. There's a jumble of things going on. Our family stands on the bank by the stairs going to the beach and watches. No one speaks. Sirens scream and fire trucks blast their horns. There's a hurt in the pit of my stomach. We sit on the bank and watch forever. Something bad has happened.

A tired looking, dripping wet guy climbs the stairs.

"You might as well go home. We're not going to find her," he says.

"Find who?" Uncle Walt asks.

"The girl," he shakes his head. "A big octopus grabbed her and pulled her under."

We eat our lunch in silence, buy a few souvenirs, and head back to Portland.

I know I'll never go in that water.

* * *

I've been raising sheep for three years. I buy school clothes with some of the money and put the rest in my savings at the bank. Daddy says I might have enough to buy a bicycle. We're going shopping. There's so many stores in Portland. How will we ever find one that sells bikes? Well, Daddy has the answer. Go to the store you trust most—Montgomery Wards.

Look at that store! It covers a whole block, and it's six high. The sign on the elevator says bikes are on the fifth floor. Wouldn't you think they'd put big stuff on the first floor so you could carry it out easier?

I've been in an elevator at home twice when I went to the dentist in the Brier Building. Dr. Klaaren's on the third floor. I'm not afraid of elevators. This one's so quiet I hardly know it's moving. Fifth floor, bicycles. I'm looking for a blue one. I can pay thirty dollars. Hope I've got enough.

"There they are," I exclaim as I bounce off the elevator. I pull Daddy's hand, wanting to go faster. "So many. How do I choose?"

"Two things," Daddy comments. "Look for one that grows with ya. It'll have a seat and bars that adjust. Then look at the price tag."

I look, I feel, I check the price; I sit in the seat. There must be a hundred bikes.

"This one," I finally decide. "It's blue and gray, but that's all right. It's pretty. It fits, it adjusts, and it's got a basket in the front so I can carry stuff. That's an extra goodie. Look at the tag, Daddy. It says $19.99. This is the one I want."

Daddy and the salesman talk about shipping. Daddy gives me my money. I pay for it.

"I'll pay for 'em to ship it on the same train we go home on, Pumpkin. Ya can git it as soon as we get off." He gives the man five dollars for shipping.

I wish I could ride it right now. I have to wait. Where in the world would you ride a bicycle in such a big city, anyway?

Sharon and her new bicycle

*   *   *

"I'm gonna take ya to the flood today." Uncle Walt tells us at breakfast. A flood? Water? Does this whole part of the world have scary water? I look at Mama and she nods her head. "It's alright," she says. "Uncle Walt will keep us safe."

"Oh my, it's bad." Aunt Frankie wrings her hands. "Killed fifteen people and none of those houses can ever be lived in again. Feel so sorry for them. I don't wanna go. It's too sad for me."

Daddy sits in front and Mama and I in the back.

"It's on the other side of Portland," Uncle tells, "right across the Columbia River from Vancouver. When they were buildin' ships down on the river during the war, lots of people came to work on them. There weren't no place for people to live so the government put up some houses real quick. They called the housing place Vanport. When the war was over, lots of workers left and went back home. Then there were black folks started moving in. They even got their own school there. 'Bout eighteen thousand people were livin' there.

I listen to Uncle Walt tell about this town, like I listen to people tell about other countries. Are these places and people real?

101

"So, on Memorial Day weekend, we got two huge rainstorms, and the temperatures got real warm. Melted the snow mighty quick in the mountains. The water was raging. Around four o'clock Memorial Day, the berm on the Spokane, Portland, Seattle Railway burst and sent a ten- foot wall of water into Vanport. People only had 'bout thirty minutes to escape. Lots of them weren't home 'cause it was a holiday. That was good. Saved lots of lives. Fifteen people didn't make it. The houses are full of mud; it's a mess. No one'll ever be able to live there again. You couldn't even see the roofs of houses when I was here two weeks ago. Let's take a look-see as how it is now." Uncle Walt turns the car up the next street, pulls to the side of the road and stops.

We're sitting high up on a hill above the flood. All I can see is water polka dotted with house roofs. We get out and walk farther to the top. Phew! It stinks horrible. Water's just sitting there, going nowhere. It looks like a huge lake of mud. I hang tight to Daddy's hand. First the scary falls, then the even scarier ocean, and now this flooded river. Yes, this place does exist. These places are real. I don't like water.

Flood at Van Port

102

Chapter 23

GRADE TROUBLES

Sharon

Third grade's tough.

"Those letters on your report card are really important." I'm told by my teacher, Miss Nichols. "A's are the best you can do 'cause nothing comes before A in the alphabet. You have to work hard to get an A."

No problem. I love learning stuff. My first report card's straight A's. Easy, peasy.

It's November first. My bus is late. Friends who walk home say, "Hey, come play with us on the playground." I've always wanted to do that. My bus comes and leaves without me.

Miss Nichols is furious. She makes me walk home to teach me a lesson. I live five miles from school. My teacher won't let me call Mama. She sends me trudging up Thain Road to Grelle.

I walk and think. I always think better when I'm moving. Yes, I've got a plan. I turn the corner at Grelle and go to Aunt Neen's house a half block down.

"Hi, Aunt Neen," I try to sound cheery. "Can I use your phone?"

"You want to use my . . .?" she looks at the driveway. "Where's your mom and dad, Sharon?"

"I missed my bus and my teacher's making me walk home. It's a long way. I want Daddy to come get me."

I'm hot in my winter coat, got a blister on my heel, and I'm almost in tears.

"Come in, come in." Neen takes my coat and I dial SH3-3612.

Mama and Daddy come real quick. Both question me. They're the ones who're furious now. My quiet talking mama calls Miss Nichols and in words and a tone of voice I've never heard from her before; lets my teacher know how she feels about what she did to me. What a mess I made. I'll never miss my bus again. I get nothing but C's for the rest of the year.

I love art. I draw a beautiful scene with mountains, a lake, and flowers. "What in the world is that?" Miss Nichols asks. "Mountains don't have sharp peaks like that. We have enough mountains around here you should know that." She gives me a C. I don't think I like those letter grades anymore.

*   *   *

I'm good friends with our school nurse, Miss Little. She really is a nurse, the kind who wears a white uniform and has a little white cap. I see her a lot. Probably 'cause we don't go to the doctor. My baby teeth are rotten. I have horrible toothaches. It's hard to concentrate on learning when your teeth hurt.

The teacher sends me to the nurse. She dips cheese cloth in oil of cloves and rubs it on my gum where the bad tooth is. In a little bit, the pain's gone and I go back to class. I'll be glad when I get my grown-up teeth.

I have tonsillitis in the winter. Miss Little takes a swab, dips it in iodine and paints my tonsils with it. No more sore throat. She's got magic for making pain go away.

When I get a cold, Mama does magic with her cough syrup. I help her make it sometimes. We cook onions 'til they're brown and gooey, put honey with it and mix it altogether with a cup of whiskey. It's always in our white cupboard by the stove. One teaspoon does the trick. No more coughing.

Miss Little came to our classroom on Monday. "Hold out a hand," she orders. "Don't eat this yet. I'll tell what it's for." She puts a Ritz cracker in each hand. She picks up an eyedropper and a brown bottle.

"In this bottle is cod-liver oil. It's good for helping your body be strong and keeps you from catching colds. I'm going to put a drop on your cracker. Then you eat it. We want you to be healthy this winter. You'll get this every Monday until April."

She drops on my cracker. I crunch away. *Mmm, not bad.* I think I'm gonna' like Mondays.

*   *   *

Miss McSorley lets me come out of class to "copy" papers for teachers when I finish my assignments 'cause I work so fast.

To make copies I put spirits (a stinky, smelly stuff) on a big orange block that looks like cheese. I put the printed paper on it, rub all over it and carefully peal it off. Then I put a clean piece of paper on it, rub it all over. Lo and behold, when I peel it off, there's the same thing on it. The smell's horrible. It takes forever to make thirty; one for each student. It's okay. I like being useful.

*   *   *

Recesses

During fall recesses my friends and I use branches to sweep leaves under the tall trees, into square and rectangle walls. We build a living room, kitchen and bedroom. Never a bathroom like rich people have 'cause we all have outhouses. We put one outhouse in the far corner by the fence. Every recess begins with "cleaning our dirt floors" from the leaves that fell last night.

"It's your turn to come visit my house," I tell my house friends. "We'll have chocolate cake and tea."

In November, the leaf fairy swoops in and they all disappear. How sad.

Two other favorite recess things are the bars and roller skating on the huge piece of cement where big kids play basketball. Mama and Daddy give me skates with a key to tighten them onto my brown oxfords for my eighth birthday. My knees and elbows are black and blue and scraped up, but I'm getting better and better.

The bars, round metal just the right size for a kid's hand, are set in concrete with gravel underneath. Two are high. I have to shimmy hand over hand up the pole to reach them. It connects three low ones to each other. I'm an expert at those. I go round and round both frontward and backward with one knee and arms hooked under the bar. I even spin around backward with both knees and my hands on the bars. I hang by my knees too, but have to do that on the tall bars or my head hits the ground. Mama makes me take pants to school to put on when I do bars, so it's okay if my dress falls over my head. Hm, maybe I should wear them skating too so I won't be so bunged up.

Today's a perfectly warm spring bar-day. I'm excited to try twelve times 'round with double knees, backwards. I jump on the low bar and call to my friends, "Count for me!" I swing hard, hear a bong, feel pain in back of my head and . . .

The next thing I know, I'm lying in the warm gravel, my head hurts horribly, and my eyes see Miss Warren's face swimming above me. "What's a teacher doing on the playground?" I wonder. Teachers are never on the playground unless someone's hurt. She's asking me questions. Her voice is far away.

The bell rings. Kids run to class. She stays until I can sit up and helps me walk in to see my friend, the school nurse. The support bar and my head had collided. I won't be doing bars for a while. This is one of those special times when the school calls your mom, and Daddy comes to take me home.

Something strange happens while I'm waiting to go home. My Jerry neighbor, whose dad rides bucking broncs, comes up to me, puts his hands on my shoulders and his lips on mine. I back away with my hands on my mouth, speechless. Why in the world would he do something like that?

You're alright," Mama says. "You've got a hard skull."

Guess she means I'm hard headed like my Daddy. It takes two weeks for my headache to go away. I never share with her about my first kiss.

*   *   *

I love the times in summer when we go fishing and huckleberry picking in the Waha Mountains. We can see those mountains from our front yard. It takes an hour to get there. One thing that scares me is the roads after we get to the General Store. They're made for loggin' trucks. They have the right of way. Sometimes when we come around a corner, there'll be a truck right there. I always pray there'll be a turnout so we can get out of its way. Once, there wasn't, and we had to back down the narrow dirt road till we could let the load of logs go by. There're stories about chains holding the logs breaking too. Logs come rolling off the truck and onto cars. I hold my breath when they go by us.

Daddy bought me a fishing pole my size. I hate waiting for fish to bite. We went fishing on the Selway river one time and I caught one. In fact, I was seven years old, and I was the only one to catch a fish that day.

Today, we're fishing at Waha. The water's ice cold. I don't see how the fish can live in that. We pick some berries, but it's not time for them to get ripe and we don't get enough for a pie.

We stop on the way home at the Waha General Store and go into the ice cave to get a Nehi Orange. It's like walking into a refrigerator. There's sawdust all over the floor, thick enough to cover up the foot part of my daddy's lace-up boots. I love the wood smell mixed with the musty smell of our dirt cellar. It's important to always shut the door of the cave to keep it cold. It's not dark. A lightbulb hangs from the ceiling. They keep beer, milk, produce and candy bars there. But Nehi Orange is my favorite.

We're almost home when I remember, "Oh no, I left my pole on a rock by the creek."

Daddy's so mad. He spins our car around and we go all the way back to the creek. It's a fast and quiet trip. It's still there. Thank goodness. I'm sorry we wasted time and gas. It's all my fault.

"I'm sorry," I say. Daddy just grunts. I don't think he believes me.

He doesn't talk to me for a week. He does that when he's mad at Mama. I'm the go- between for them. He'll say, "Sharon, tell your mother . . ." even if she's standing right there. I don't understand why. Now he's done it to me. I love Daddy. I want him to talk to me. I don't know what to do. I'll try harder to think and do the right thing and take care of my stuff.

Chapter 24

CAMP MEETING

Tom

Wells, never 'spected I'd be doin' this. Susie's cousin, Elmer Swineheart, gave her an invite to The Church of God Camp Meetin' up by Colfax. They calls it "The Saints Home." Huh! Saints. Like they're perfect and proud. Not met a saint yet. All got dirty halos. Heard 'bout this place when I's a kid. We didn't go. Too far. Horses wouldn't make it pullin' nine peoples up that hill. Heard 'bout loud preachin', gettin' healed, gettin' saved, baptizin' in the crick. Not good memories. Make's me shudder.

Older sisses, Neen and Grace went thar with sum friends. Now they're on my back ta go too. Three weeks it's been. Nag, nag, nag. I gave up. We'll go. But just for a day. Too much work waitin' at home. Hope the ol' car'll make up up the hill.

* * *

Susan

Tom's sister Frankie's here visiting. They're thinking of moving back to this area because Walt's gone a lot on road construction. It would be nice for Tom to have his two brothers and three sisters close by.

The sisters are begging Tom to go to the Church of God Camp meeting at Colfax. I'm not sure they're going to succeed. Tom's family attended this church in Stites, Idaho; the church where his dad acted all religious and pious on Sunday mornings, then beat Tom all week. Can't say I blame him for being defiant and resentful when we call God our Father. Why should he want to go to a place where all they do is talk about rules for living and the wrath of God? He's had enough wrath to last a lifetime. I'm praying hard; praying that if he does go, they'll talk about God's love, not punishment.

Oh, here come the sisters now. "Hello, girls," I call.

They pile out of Neen's Model A Ford. It's a tight fit. They're big ladies.

"Hi, Susie." Frankie greats me with a hug. "Good to see you, again."

"Where's that brother of ours?" Grace asks.

"He's out moving the water on the alfalfa field. He should be in soon. Come have some lemonade. It's pretty hot today, isn't it? Hasn't rained for two weeks so we're having to water all the time." They sit while I pour freshly squeezed lemonade.

Neen glances up at me. "Have you been praying, Susie? We've got to get him to go. He needs to have Jesus in his heart."

"Of course, I have. Constantly, from the day I discovered how much he hates God," I answer. "Thanks for trying to persuade him."

Tom comes in, stomping mud off his boots on the porch. "Well, if it isn't the three musketeers," he exclaims. "Come to harass the brother again, have you?"

"Now Tom, we're just concerned. We want what's best for you," Frankie responds.

"Alls we're asking is that you drive up for the day. What's it's gonna hurt?" Grace questions.

"I've been thinkin'. If it'll get you off my back, we'll go. Not until Thursday cause I have Thursday and Friday off." Tom grouches trying to be mad, but with a smile. "I can't fight three sisters, a wife, and daughter. I give."

My heart's suddenly light. I'm singing inside, thanking God. Now I'll just keep praying for the preacher.

Thursday morning we leave early. I'm thrilled. I've heard so much about this Camp Meeting. Daddy A. F. Gray, who came to our schoolhouse when I was sixteen to preach, is going to be the preacher at Camp Meeting. It was after one of his sermons I let Jesus take over my life. Sharon's excited too.

Going up the Lewiston Hill's an adventure. The campground's about forty-five miles away, almost to Colfax. Halfway up the steep, windy grade, Tom pulls over to stop at a spring piped out of the rocks. Cars can't go up this hill without overheating. Everyone stops to put water in the radiator and cool the engine.

Sharon and I fill a jug with the cold, cold water and lug it back to Tom. He opens the hood and steam hisses out as he uses an old rag to open the cap slowly. It's a good thing God put this spring here.

In two hours, we're at the campground. It's just as I imagined. There's an old church nestled against a cliff connected by a wooden sidewalk to a big dining hall. The bottom of the dining hall has sleeping quarters for people who stay the week. Evidently there are not enough rooms. On the other side of the church is a row of tents. Most of them old army tents like we lived in on the Stick Ranch. Memories rattle my brain.

Down below on the "flat" by the creek is a huge white canvas tent. Sharon's pulling on my hand. "Come on, Mama, I want to see the tent."

"Go ahead," I say. "We'll be there in a moment." I glance over my shoulder and see Tom still in the car. "Are you coming?" I holler.

"I'll wait for the girls. You go ahead with Sharon," he calls back as he pulls out a cigarette and lights it.

I nod, head for the tent and pray he doesn't stay in the car all day. When I step into the tent, I feel the hush of my steps in the five inches of coarse sawdust. It's amazingly cool inside. It's dim. My eyes adjust, and I spy Sharon sitting on the first bench in front of a little stage and pulpit. I sit quietly beside her. There's a reverent feel about this place.

After a long silence, Sharon takes my hand and says, "Are you praying for Daddy too?" I nod.

*   *   *

Sharon

Campmeeting

Camp Meeting feels like home. It must be something like heaven's gonna be. Everybody's smiling, happy to see us, gives hugs. The best part is sitting in the tent when it's empty. I can feel my invisible Jesus sitting beside me. The smell of the sawdust all over the floor is like being in the ice cave on Waha mountain. It's quiet and peaceful in here.

People come in and sit quietly, even kids. Some are praying, I think. Two men walk up to the front on the little stage. One says, "Turn to page five." I can hear pages turning and look at Mama. She goes to the back door to get a songbook. When she comes back, my aunts come with her—and my daddy. Now we're all here.

The singing starts. Oh, how they sing. No piano, just voices. Some high, some low, all mixed together. "I have washed my robes in the cleansing fountain, I am a child of God." Oh, yes, this is what heaven's gonna be like. I glance up at Mama and see tears on her cheeks, like when I told her I asked Jesus to be in me.

After the service is over, we get in line on the wood sidewalk that goes to the big dining hall. Mmm, you can smell the food cooking.

"Smells like roast," Aunt Neen says. "Everybody donates. A hundred and fifty people's a lot to feed. Hafta have more than five loaves and two fish in this day and age."

She's right. Inside's a jar where Daddy puts three, dollar bills. We find a long empty bench where our family can all sit. On the table is butter, baskets of bread, big bowls of coleslaw and pitchers of juice. We have a glass, plate and silverware. An older kid plops a bowl of potatoes and a huge platter of meat in the middle of our table. Someone starts to sing, "Praise God from whom all blessings flow . . ." After the amen, the food's passed around and we eat till we're stuffed. The servers bring a bowl of chocolate pudding. Oh, where will I put that? I think. But I find a little corner in my tummy.

"Can I see the kitchen?" I ask Mama.

"We'll peek in as we go out. We can't go in. They'll be doing dishes. We don't want to be in their way."

Three huge wood stoves! Can you imagine cooking on three stoves? Three cooks clean up the stoves. One cuts up lettuce for supper's salad. Oh my, I wonder how they do that? Do they ever get to rest? At the other end, older kids wash dishes. Outside, two boys cut wood for the stoves. It's hard work to feed a camp meeting.

Outside, people put blankets on the ground, sit and visit. There's a class for kids five to twelve in the church building. I make two new friends, Gordon and LaRae. We sing too. These people sing everywhere. I hear men singing outside and down in the tent, people sing like our church choir.

Gordon and LaRae came with their mama. My mama knew her when she was a kid at Reubens. After class, my new friends take me to the creek. I find a frog, but I'm not fast enough to catch him. There's little fish and snails in the water, and even a crawdad. I find two pretty rocks I slip in my pocket.

"Let's go watch the game," Gordon says. "I can't play. It's just for old kids, but I like to watch."

We wade across the creek to the flat field and watch. I think baseball's boring unless you get to play.

We spend the rest of the afternoon exploring. It's too bad there's only big pine trees. Their limbs are too high to reach. I don't see a single climbing tree in this whole place. Not even small pine trees like at Waha. I love to climb to the top of small ones and hang on for dear life while Daddy pulls the top of it way down and lets go. It's like riding a bucking horse, flippin' and floppin'.

"Ding, ding, ding." We hear the big dinner bell by the dining hall. This is good, I'm thinking. I'm starved. I find my family and stand in line. This time we sing our thank you song outside. Waiting for us on the long tables are sandwiches, salads, and applesauce. I make mine disappear quick.

People finish eating and head to the tent. We hear the singing while we're still in the dining hall. They love to sing—loud and long. Daddy Gray talks again. I'm so tired. I lean against my daddy and fall asleep.

I don't know how I got in the car or remember the ride home. I do know I want to go back there again.

Chapter 25

FAMILY VISITING

Denney family

Sharon

Mama Grew up on a farm close to Reubens. It's still in the state of Idaho, even though we drive an hour and a half to get there. We go there on little trips—up the hill in the early morning and back to home in the evening. We visit with Mama's Aunt Elma, Uncle Arlo, Uncle Alva, Aunt Juni, and Uncle Ope.

Uncle Ope runs the Reuben's Pool Hall. I get to go there by myself and visit cause it's only at the other end of the alley from their house. There's sawdust on the floor and a long high counter with stools that spin around like the fountain at our grocery store. Uncle Ope always gives me a Nehi Orange. Sometimes men sit at a table playing cards. Sometimes they play a game they call pool. Guess that's why they call it a pool hall. Everyone's always nice to me. If I smile pretty, one of them might buy me an ice cream cone.

We go to see Aunt Phoebe, too. She runs the post office and the big hotel. Aunt Elma helps her out. There's a great big kitchen with a long, long table. I help Mama set the table, and the hotel guests, the aunts, and we eat together. Daddy knows 'bout everyone eatin' there 'cause they all work for the Camus Prairie Railroad. They bring the train up from Lewiston, stay all night at the hotel, then take the train back in the morning. People ride the train and ship packages and letters up and down too.

Aunt Phoebe and Aunt Elmi set food on the table. Everybody's talking and laughing. It's like a big happy family. An extra treat is to play the pump organ in the living room. It's loud, so I don't get to play it much.

We make a trip to the cemetery and put flowers on Mama's grandma and grandpa's graves before we leave. She's got good memories and tells lots of stories about them while we're there.

*   *   *

The other family we visit belongs to Daddy, so they're a Chase. They're his aunt and uncle, so Mama says they're my great aunt and uncle. That means they're really old. We turn left on a farm road outside of Cottonwood and then another left, then turn right. We've been here so many times I know exactly where to go. If it's harvest season, we have to watch for trucks hauling grain. It's a dirt road full of holes from those big trucks.

Uncle John and Aunt Perna live in a farmhouse on a hill above an old schoolhouse. No one goes to school there anymore, so Uncle John owns it. It still has a swing, a slide, and a merry-go- round. That's the place I go while the grown-ups visit. I always get sick on that merry-go-round, no matter how hard I try not to. But I love it.

There's a creek too. It's about as big as the one we fish in at Waha. There's a bridge that goes across it just beyond the schoolhouse. I love to stand on it and watch the water swish under it. I never get in it. Water scares me.

Uncle John's over sixty, but he still has cattle in the pasture across the road. There's a cow in the barn too, and sheep. Aunt Purna spins wool into yarn and makes hats, scarves, and socks. She tries to teach me to spin. I'm too slow. She can do it fast, fast, fast. Of course, there're chickens, geese, and pigs. They have a well. The ice-cold water makes yummy lemonade.

Aunt Purna's a tiny lady. I'm taller than she is. She's a great cook. She buzzes around her wood stove and whips up a meal in no time. There's always pie for dessert.

"Come on, Sharon," she says, "let's you and me sneak down to the chicken coop and see if the old hens left us a gift." I get to carry her wire basket. She lets me feed the chickens while we're there. Sometimes I climb up the ladder and pick apples off the old tree. I help peel them for a pie. I can tell she really loves kids. Her kids and grandkids live a ways off, so I get to be her kid for a while.

Daddy told me Uncle John built their house all by himself. When you walk in the front door, you're in a big living room. I bet twelve people could sit in it. Most of the floor is covered by a braided rug like Mrs. Vandell's. Aunt Purna tells me stories about the pieces she used to make hers. There's a long leather couch and a huge leather chair where Uncle John always sits, two rocking chairs, three arm chairs, and two stools. Yep, it could hold a dozen people.

The other side of this big room, on the back end of the house, is a long table. It could hold twelve people too. You see, when the Chases get together there's lots of 'em. On the other back side is a kitchen with a big, black, wood stove, counters, and a two-sided sink. On the front side of the kitchen is their bedroom.

Uncle John's a storyteller. We sit in the living room after supper; the air buzzes with all kinds of stories. I cuddle up on the leather couch next to Mama and listen until I'm about to fall asleep. Aunt Purna takes me upstairs to the big room with four beds. I always choose the one close to the stairs so I can still hear stories. She helps me into my jammies, says my prayers with me, and tucks me into the soft squishy bed with the crackly, thick, down quilt she's made from goose feathers. I listen and fall asleep dreamin' about mule packin' on hunting trips, dogs fightin' a bear, shooting the biggest elk ever, and it took five men to haul it out of the draw.

Uncle John and Aunt Purna are like the Grandma and Grandpa Chase I never got to know 'cause they died before I had a memory. All Chases love them and they love us right back.

Tom and Uncle John

Chapter 26

BAD AND WATER

Sharon

I've got to talk about doing bad and water. Those are words we never talk about in my house, but when you've got neighbors with eleven kids, they talk about it like they talk about supper. You see it and smell it all the time. Yuck.

So, what's it all about? This is what I know. We all do it and it's private, except for babies who wear diapers.

I'm playing at Snyder's. They have a new baby—they always have a new baby. There's eleven kids at their house now. Emma brings Glenna in the living room, puts her on the davenport and says to Louise, "Your turn."

Louise unpins the diaper. Oh, man is it stinky, has runny brown goo, and well, I can't even tell how awful it is. I stare. Louise puts the mess on the floor and starts washing the baby with a washrag and pan of water.

What's she gonna' do with that diaper? I keep thinking. I watch as she puts a clean cloth back on Glenna and puts her back in the sleeping basket. She picks up the dirty cloth, drops it in the pan, and walks outside with it. *Is she gonna' throw it away?* I watch through the window. She goes to the flower bed, sloshes the diaper up and down in the pan a few times and dumps it on the flowers. Then she takes the hose, sprays the cloth, wrings it out like Mama does clothes on wash day, drops it back in the pan and puts it on the back porch by the wash machine. I bet they have to wash more than just Mondays.

"Whatcha looking at?" Louise asks me when she comes back in. "Never seen a diaper changed before?"

"Uh, no." I shake my head.

"Everybody's got bad in 'em. Even babies. It's leftovers of what we eat. It's gotta come out."

"Like when we water?" I ask. She nods.

"When does bad happen?" I can't look her in the eye 'cause I'm embarrassed. After all, I'm nine years old and I should know these things.

"Depends how often and what you eat," she says. "You don't know much, do you? You need to get a baby at your house." She laughs.

I know now, I say to myself. I don't think I want a baby at my house. I don't want to clean up a mess like that.

I wonder, *How did Mama do that? I was born in winter. Water freezes. How did she clean the cloth?*

Mama and I walk up across the alfalfa field to our house. "Mama, did you see Louise change the baby?"

"Yes," Mama says. "She's old enough to help take care of the baby."

"How did you clean my diapers?" I question.

"Winter was easier," Mama replies. "I rinsed them out in the wash pan, like Louise did, and put them on the back porch. They froze there until wash day. Grandma made enough flannel diapers so I could usually get through till Mondays."

"Then you just threw them in the wash machine?"

"With a bar of my lye soap. It took out stains and smells. The hard part was making sure I rinsed them enough to get the soap out so it wouldn't burn your skin." Mama sighed. "I sure had red hands that winter. Between rinsing out lye and hanging them on the line before they froze again, my poor hands were like raw meat. The diapers froze dry on the line like our sheets and clothes do now."

"Uh . . . uh, Mama?"

"Yes?"

"How come I don't wear a diaper now?"

Mama chuckles. "Well, you were trained by the time you were a year old."

"Trained?" I asked.

"You went to the outhouse," she answered.

"Oh."

I remember a time when my mama went to the outhouse with me to do it. I'm glad 'cause the holes were so big I was afraid I'd fall in. She showed me how to tear out pages from the catalogue, magazines or newspapers and crumple them up to wipe down there. When I was about four, Mama quit coming with me. I still sit on the edge. My worst nightmare's falling in.

At night, we have a potty in the bedroom. It has a lid, so it doesn't smell too bad. I'm glad it's dark so no one can see me. In the morning, I have to dump it in the outhouse on my first trip.

When it's hot out, Mama takes the hose and washes the inside of our outhouse. In the winter she dumps lime down the two holes and uses a pan of hot water with lye to wash the seats.

It's lots of work to take care of our "toilet," as Mama starts calling it.

"Where's Daddy?" I ask.

"Out digging a new hole for the toilet."

"A new hole? Is the old one full?"

"Not quite, but we have to dig a new one about every four or five years."

"I'm gonna watch." I run out the back door.

Daddy's in a hole up to his knees already, a ways back of our old toilet between the barn and the chicken coop. He's put four sticks in the ground to make the corners, so it's not too big for the little house.

"Oh, it's deep already!" I yell.

"Long ways ta go," he says. "It'll be deeper than I'm tall."

"Oh, dear. How will you get out?"

"The ladder," he replies.

It takes two days for Daddy to finish digging. He brings home buckets of gravel and pours it in the hole. Three friends come, help lift our toilet onto logs and roll it to the new hole. It smells good in there 'cause there's no bad in it. Our family never talks about water or bad. It's a very private thing, but everybody does it.

$\mathscr{C}hapter\ 27$

GROCERIES

Walker's store

Susan

"Come on, Sharon. Let's get to the store before it gets too hot." I call her in from the backyard where she's feeding her sheep.

"Can I ride my bike?" she asks.

"No, that's too far and I'm too slow. I want you to stay with me," I answer. I've never learned to drive. Even if I knew how, Tom always takes the car to work now that gas isn't rationed.

Walker's store is on the corner of 18th and Grelle. We live in the middle of the twentieth block. It doesn't sound far, but each block is a quarter of a mile long in the Orchards. It's not like we can run to the store every day. Besides, we raise most of our own food. I'm out of flour and tomorrow is baking day. Don't know how I didn't notice before we went to town last Saturday. That's where we get most of the groceries we need to buy.

There's also Knepper's store. That's five miles away. It's the place where we rent our meat locker. When we butcher, we take the carcass to them. They cut it into our order, wrap it, and put it in our locker. They even grind up some of it for hamburger and make sausage. For years we cut up our meat on our kitchen table and wrapped it. It's hard work using the bone saw and butcher knife. It only costs five cents a pound to have Kneppers do it. They have an electric saw that makes the work easier. Sure nice to have someone do it for us.

A little grocery wagon comes three days a week. It beeps its horn. If we need anything, we run out and stand on the end of the driveway. They carry basics plus ice cream bars, candy and pop. I buy from them sometimes. Things cost more. They've got to pay for their gas.

The Nez Perce people come by our house with salmon to sell during fishing season at Celilo Falls. Tom and I buy at least two, cut them up and put them in the locker. We like to help them out and we get a treat.

Sharon skips ahead of me, singing. Suddenly she stops and stares beside the road.

"What do you see, honey?" I walk over to where she's squatted down. There's a tiny bird sitting in the grass.

"I think he's been hit by a car. Can I take him home and be a nurse to him?" she questions.

"Let's leave him there until we come back. If he's still there, you can take him home."

Sharon has a kind heart for small helpless creatures.

The old folk Walkers are slowing turning over the store to their daughter and her husband. It's a small store with creaky floors and tight aisles. There's only two or three items of each thing. They carry whatever the neighborhood might need in a pinch. It's not a place where you'd go to do all your shopping. Nice friendly folks.

"Hi, there, Chases. How are you doing? Nice day for a walk."

"We found a bird beside the road," explains Sharon. "I think it got hit by a car."

"I'm so sorry." Mable shakes her head. "Cars and birds don't get along good in the same place."

"I'm going to take it home and make it better," Sharon declares.

Packing ten pounds of flour a half mile uphill is a definite challenge. Sharon watches carefully for the bird. We had put a white hanky beside it so it would be easy to spot. The hanky's there, but the bird's gone.

"Guess it got well on its own," she declares. I can tell she's disappointed, yet happy.

Chapter 28

THE CIRCUS COMES TO TOWN

Sharon

I run home as fast as I can from the bus stop. Lassie sits on the edge of the lawn waiting for me. She's always glad to see me, but never comes out on the road. I give her a pat and a hug and run on to the house.

"Mama, Mama," I yell before I even get the door open. "There's a circus coming to Lewiston the week after school's out. Can we go? Can we? It's called Barnum and Bailey Circus and it has elephants and tigers and high wire acts where people walk on a rope and . . ."

"Whoa. Slow down. I can't understand a thing you're saying," Mama says. "Take a big breath."

I do.

"Now start over."

I tell her all about the circus. Kids in my class talked about it all day. I've never been to a circus.

"They said there'll even be a parade, and we can go down to the beach on the Snake River and watch them set up the circus tent."

"We'll have to talk to Daddy about it when he comes back from getting oats for the cow." She always asks him what he thinks.

If he says, "We'll see," it means yes.

They talk it over and the answer is yes! I can hardly stand it. It's ten whole days away. Days move slow.

Finally, it's time. On Friday, they set up the tents. We drive down to a street called Prospect and park. On the hill, we can watch the men and elephants work. I thought elephants were wild animals. I didn't know they help people just like horses and mules. Really, they're even better 'cause they can pick up the big poles in their trunk. It would take a lot of men to do that. We watch them put up the huge red and white striped tent where the show's gonna be. We leave 'cause chores have to be done before Daddy goes to work. Tomorrow's the parade.

*　　*　　*

It was hard to sleep last night. The parade starts at nine o'clock. Daddy gets home from work at seven. We have breakfast and go to town. We're early, so we get a good spot. Everyone's excited and talking. This is a big deal in our town. Everybody's here.

I hear music. "They're coming, they're coming," I jump up and down. The circus band comes first. They're dressed in red coats with gold trim and black pants. Boy, are they loud. I cover my ears as they go by.

Next is acrobats. They do all kind of things I wish I could do. Their bodies look like rubber as they twist and turn. There're clowns with way-too-big clothes, little tiny people, beautiful girls on horses doing tricks down the street, a guy with trained dogs doing tricks too. And then—oh yes—then come the cages. Three cages have lions who roar and scare me. Sure glad they can't get out. Two cages have tigers who look like they're tired and just want a nap. Last of all are the elephants in a long line from the biggest to the smallest. Each one holds onto the tail of the one in front of him. All I can do is giggle. What a parade! This afternoon we go to the circus.

Daddy takes a long nap so he won't be tired for the show. I get paper and draw pictures of the parade. It was the best parade ever.

*　　*　　*

The tent's on the other side of the railroad tracks. Since the circus travels by train, that's handy for them. We stand in line to get tickets. While we're waiting, Mama goes to a cart and buys some hot in-the-shell peanuts. She says we need them for later.

"Ooh, look at the rings in the middle of the tent," I yell as we enter the Big Top. "Now I know why they call it that. It's the biggest tent I've ever seen." The floor's covered with sawdust and it gets in my shoes and makes my feet itch.

"Where do you want to sit?" Mama asks as we look at the benches that get taller and taller.

"Up high, up there. Not all the way. I want to be tall so I can see." I climb. We settle in and wait.

A clown comes and acts funny, so we have something to laugh at while we wait. He stomps up the benches with his huge feet and stops in front of me. He points at me, at the red flower on his bright blue coat, and touches my nose.

"You want me to smell your flower?" I ask. His head goes up and down. I stand and put my nose on the flower.

"Oh," I cry out as I get squirted in the face with water from the flower. Everyone laughs, except me. I can't believe he'd do that to me. Mama gives me a hanky to wipe my face. She's smiling. I think I'm the "butt of a joke."

The circus band marches in playing and sits on the other side of the tent. A man in a black suit and tall, black hat comes to the center ring and announces, "Ladies and gentlemen, boys and girls, please stand for the national anthem."

We do. I can sing it too, 'cause we do it in school.

"You may be seated. Welcome to the Barnum and Bailey Circus. Today we will treat you to only the best in entertainment. May I introduce our cast."

Suddenly, the side flaps pull back and in comes a huge elephant with a lady riding in his curled trunk. She must trust him a lot. Behind them comes everybody we saw this morning and then some. They go around the outside of the rings next to the people. I'm glad we're not in the front rows. I'd be afraid. The tall hat man shouts out the names as they come in. There's so many. They all go out.

Tall Hat announces, "And now, let the show begin."

I stare. If I blink, I'll miss something. So many acts. So many animals I've never seen. So many things I didn't know people could do. The most exciting act, he calls the flying trapeze. I love the bars at school. These flying bars hang from the ceiling and swing. People do somersaults from them and jump from their swing to the person on the other swing. It looks like the most fun thing in the world. I decide that's what I want to do when I grow up. I clap and cheer for all the acts, but the flying trapeze makes screams come out of me.

As we get ready to leave, Mama hands me the bag of peanuts. I'll eat them on the way home. We don't go right to the car. We go in back of the tent where the animals live in their cages to get a closeup look. At the end of the row, a man sits on a little red stool. A monkey sits next to him on a yellow stool.

"Hi there," he says, looking down at me. "What's your name?"

"Sharon," I answer.

"Well, isn't that a coincidence?" he smiles. "I'd like you to meet my friend, Sharon." He points at the monkey. "She's like one of my family and loves peanuts. You wouldn't happen to have one?"

I look quick at Mama. She smiles. I hold out a peanut. The monkey smiles and takes it. She's good at getting it out of the shell. I give her two more. She pats my hand and smiles.

It's time to head home.

I can't talk about anything but the trapeze. I try to imagine what it feels like to fly through the air. I can do it. I'm not afraid to go high. I climb our two big shade trees clear to the top. I walk across limbs up there just hanging on to little branches to keep my balance. I know I could do a trapeze.

The next week Daddy surprises me with a metal bar hanging by chains on one of the big shade tree limbs. I have a trapeze of my own! I can practice and practice.

*　　*　　*

Mama and Daddy make big changes in our kitchen. They paint it bright Dutch Blue with Canary Yellow trim; get rid of the icebox and put in a refrigerator; take out the wood cookstove and put in an electric stove. They put metal cabinets with a sink all across the wall under the big, new window that slides over, instead of up.

I wonder how Daddy's going to shoot pheasants out that window. It's high—up above the sink. The old window was low enough Daddy could sit in a chair, raise the window and shoot those birds eating his just-planted corn seeds. Maybe we won't have pheasant dinner anymore.

There's been a lot of taking and putting, and this doesn't look like our kitchen anymore.

"Now I've got to learn to cook all over again," Mama says. I know she'll do it. She can cook anywhere on anything. I'll miss the slices of potato fried on top of the wood stove, though.

Chapter 29

BIRDS DON'T FLY, AND STAMPS DO BUY

Green Stamps

Sharon

My friend Sylvia's mom is a Blue Bird leader. I've never heard of that gang. She says I'd love it. Mama gives me two dollars. I sign up to be in Mrs. Nassett's Blue Bird group. On Tuesday after school, I walk home with Sylvia.

"Do we learn to fly?" I ask.

"No, silly," she laughs.

"Then why do they call us Blue Birds?"

"Who knows. I've never learned to fly," she tells me.

Her house is bigger than ours. It's a good thing, 'cause there's twelve girls here. We sit in a circle on the living room floor and sing the Blue Bird song, stand and say the Pledge of Allegiance, and pray. There's a Blue Bird Pledge too. I don't know anything about Bird Pledges, so I just listen.

"It's time to work on badges," Mrs Nassett says. "Sharon, since this is your first time here, you work with Vicky. She'll help you learn the song and pledge and tell you what we do."

Everyone else goes around tables and starts to work on "projects." Vicky takes me in the kitchen. We sit at the table. I really want to be with the rest of them. Vicky says I have to know this stuff first. Okay, I'm bored. I've asked her three times if we're going to learn to fly, and she just laughs. I think she's laughing at me and that makes me feel funny inside.

I hear my daddy's voice, "Is Sharon ready to come home?"

I grab my school stuff and run out to meet him. "I'm ready to come home," I shout.

I never go back 'cause I don't think they'll teach me how to fly.

* * *

Green Stamps

I don't remember a time when we didn't get green stamps. They're the same size as stamps Mama puts on her letters, except they're bright green and have S&H in the middle of them. When we buy gas, groceries, or even clothes, the clerks always ask if we collect stamps. Our answer is yes.

It's my job to put those stamps in the little book of blank pages with lines just the right size for rows. They taste terrible, so Mama gives me a wet rag to paste them in.

"Another book's full," I call to Mama.

"Oh good," she answers. "That makes three full books. Now we can get a new toaster. Won't it be nice to have toast again?"

Our toaster was ancient. The sides went down; you put the bread on it and flip them up, then plugged it in. You watched carefully, and when that side was brown, you let down the doors, turned the bread over and waited till it was brown on the other side. The cord was made out of cloth. Before Christmas, it caught fire when Daddy plugged it in. Scary. Yes, it'll be nice to have toast again.

On Saturday, we go to the Green Stamp place in the basement of the Idaho Department Store to look at stuff we can buy. There's a shiny, silver toaster and it costs three books of stamps. Perfect. Mama always knows exactly how many she needs 'cause she has a stamp catalogue.

"This is just what we need," Mama says to the lady behind the counter. The lady goes in the back room and comes out with a box that says toaster on it. She takes our books and makes a black X across each page.

"Fifty cents, please." The lady tells us. Mama says we pay a little bit so the store can pay her. I think I'd like to have a job here. They're always nice to us.

Mama has other things she got with Green Stamps too: blankets, pillows, and a yellow, electric mixer. It makes mashed potatoes fast. My most favoritest thing of all is the blue stool. It's made out of iron, heavy and tall. So tall that an adult can sit on it and dangle their feet. I have to climb up on the bars around the bottom to get up there.

The blue stool sits in our kitchen by the counter. Mama uses it when she's peeling apples for making applesauce or cutting up peaches and apricots for canning. She says it "saves her back." I use it for talking.

When I get home from school, Mama always has a snack waiting for me on the counter by the blue stool. I climb up there and nibble away.

"How was your day?" Mama asks. I spend the next half hour telling her all the things that happened and what I learned, while she's busy getting supper on the stove or in the oven. My mama's always working in the kitchen. Sometimes I watch and sometimes she lets me help. But I can't talk about my day if I'm helping. It's like the blue stool is magic and makes me talk and talk.

Chapter 30

FOURTH GRADE BLUES

Sharon

1949

There's a huge change in my life. The Orchards school doesn't have room for everyone. They ship us fourth graders downtown to the old Webster school by the high school. Daddy says the Lewiston Orchards has grown so much, the school district's building another school on the west side. I don't like it. I have friends I won't see all year. Some friends in fourth grade will move to the new school when they get it built. I'm mad and sad.

"Life can't stay the same," Mama explains. "It's like a river. When the river gets full, the water has to find another place to run. We just have to go with the flow." Mama's wise. I trust her. My first flow is the long, ten-mile bus ride. I need to get up a half hour earlier.

My teacher, Miss Graves, is young, as short as the tallest boy in our class, and wears black- rimmed glasses. Her high voice grates like a fingernail on the chalkboard. When she gets mad, she's loud and squeaky and I want to cover my ears. She doesn't like boys. She's sends them to a corner of the room to do their work. They sit on the floor with their back to the class. Her name fits. I never see her smile.

"Jimmy," Miss Graves squeaks, "what's in your mouth?"

"Gum, Miss Graves." He answers with a smirk on his face. "The doctor . . ."

"Stand on your desk," she shouts. "Go on, climb on your desk and stand up."

We stare. What in the world's happening? We'd be in big trouble if we stood on our desk. It wobbles and doesn't look safe 'cause these desks aren't bolted down.

"Take your gum out. Put it on your nose," she commands.

Kids giggle, but stop quick when she looks daggers at them.

"Everyone, get back to work."

Of course, Jimmy can't work.

I bury my face in math, but glance often to see if Jimmy's okay. Sometimes he blanks out. Mama told me his mind sort of freezes. It's called seizures. He's the tallest boy in our class, and it's a long way to the floor if he loses his balance. I glance at the clock. It's been fifteen minutes. He's beginning to sway.

"How much longer?" Jimmy asks.

"I'll tell you when," she snips.

I finish my assignment and take out my writing tablet. I keep a close eye on my friend who's standing on his desk right in front of me. He's looking straight ahead, balancing the gum, swaying. I see him starting to topple, jump from my desk, grab his legs and hold him. Yes, he's having a seizure.

"Sharon!" I hear her yelling my name. "Sit down or you'll be up there too."

I hang on tight, ignoring her demand. Bobby helps, and we carefully let him down to the floor. He lies there, eyes open and not moving. Miss Graves stomps toward us, red faced. We move quickly away. The class stares at her. How could she be so cruel?

"Get up," she orders Jimmy. There's no movement from Jimmy or anyone else in the room. "I said, get up!" Still no response. I glance up and watch her face turn white. She throws her hands over her mouth and rushes from the room. We wait. As his friends, we breathe for Jimmy, wanting him to take the big breath we know will bring him out of this.

A man rushes into the room. "Get back, students." He kneels down and strokes Jimmy's face and talks to him. There's a breath, then a bigger breath. Jimmy blinks his eyes.

Miss Graves doesn't come back that day or the next. On Monday, she's quiet but never apologizes.

*   *   *

In third grade, Mr. Woods came to class and taught us how to play Tonettes and read music notes. I loved that. His high school band room is on the fourth floor of old Webster School. They practice every day at two o'clock. The sounds of drums, horns, flutes and clarinets float down the stairs and into our room. I toe-tap along as I read my geography book.

In October, Mr. Woods comes into our room with some instruments.

"Students," he begins, "I'd like to teach you how to play an instrument." He demonstrates and tells how each is played. I like the sound of the clarinet. "Next Friday, you'll come to the band room and try them out for yourself. Talk to your parents about joining fourth grade band. If you like it, you can continue all the way through school till you graduate. I have some instruments your parents can rent and a few you can buy. I'll see you next Friday."

Boy, this is exciting news.

On Friday, I try the clarinet, the flute, and the saxophone. My cousin, Patty, plays the saxophone. I like it, but it's way too big to carry around. I still like the clarinet best.

I jump off the bus, run home and beg Mama and Daddy, "Can I? Can I?"

"We'll see." Daddy gives his pat answer. Remember, that means yes. "We'll go meet with Mr. Woods."

Of course, the answer's yes. In fact, they buy a special clarinet. It's black and has Benny Goodman's name carved in the bell. He's the greatest clarinet player ever. He even has his own orchestra. We listen to it on the radio. My instrument fits in a brown case along with reeds, cleaning cloth, extra pads, and the little brown book we'll use. I'm going to be a clarinet player. I proudly carry my little case and tread up the creaky stairs to the band room.

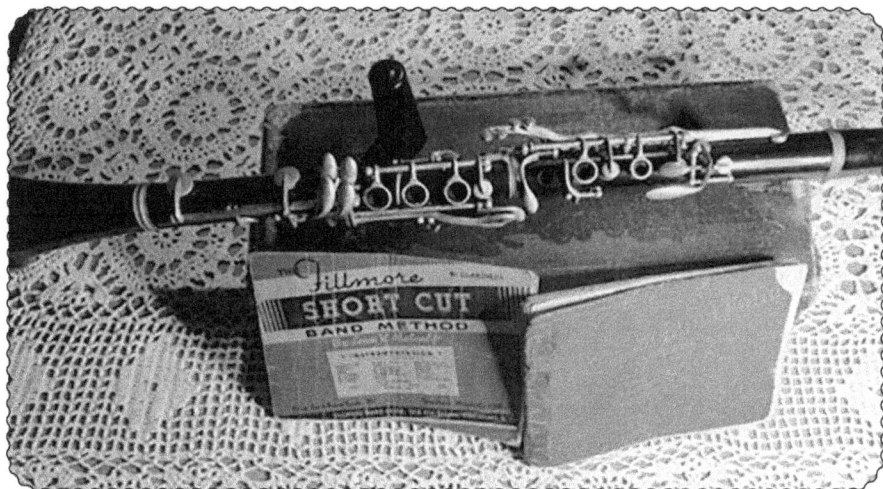

Clarinet and books

Band's not the only music thing happening in fourth grade. All one hundred and twenty-six fourth graders in Lewiston do a song and dance about a rainbow in a play called "Indian Summer" at the high school. Grades ten through twelve act out the story. We fourth graders are a village of Indians they visit. We entertain them. We practice and practice on the big stage at the high school auditorium. We just walk across the street to get there.

After the performance everyone says, "You did good."

I've no idea what the story's about. No one ever explains it. We never get to see the whole play. It's my first time in a thing they call drama.

*   *   *

In the Orchard's Community Church basement where we have children's church, there's a piano. I love plunking out tunes on it. I hear if I should go up or down. I stay as long as Mama lets me, trying to pick out songs. Sandy likes the piano too. She hogs it when she's there. One day I get tired of her not letting me have a turn. I reach down and pull the stool from out from under her. She falls on her bottom and cries. I have to ask Jesus to forgive me. Sandy, too. I'm embarrassed and sorry

I hurt someone. This is the second time. Remember the teeter totter? Why in the world do I do stuff like that?

* * *

Can of marbles

This old building wasn't made for fourth graders. It used to be a big kid's school. There's nothing to play on at recess. We're tired of playing tag and guessing games.

"Hey, look at that place where cars park." I show my friends. "We can play marbles. I still have mine I bought in a grab bag at Newberry's when I was a little kid."

I play marbles with my daddy, but not much at school. At the Orchard's school, we drew rings with a stick in the dirt to play. We had to pack it down hard cause marbles don't roll good in dirt. This place is perfect. We need chalk to draw the circles. I have some I use for my front yard school in summer.

In case you've never played marbles, here are the rules:

> Make a circle on the ground about three feet wide.
> Each kid puts the same number of marbles inside the circle toward the middle.

Choose a big marble to be your shooter.

Decide if you're playing for keeps or for fair. In fair, everyone takes their own marbles at the end of the game. In keeps you keep all the marbles you knock out of the circle.

Kneel outside the circle with your hand on the edge of the ring, put your shooter in your hand so your thumb can shoot it. Try to do it hard enough to knock other marbles out of the center.

If your shooter stops in the middle, it has to stay there. You get to shoot at the other marbles from where it is. That's dangerous, cause if someone else knocks your shooter out, they win the game. Otherwise, games are over when all the marbles are knocked out.

This will be a great chance to beat the boys. They think they're so good.

Mama triple stitches a little bag for my marbles. I fill it with a piece of chalk and my beautiful marbles plus a couple of steelies. Those are little round steel marbles from machines, Daddy gives me. They do lots of damage to glass marbles if you hit 'em too hard.

Off I go to conquer the marble kingdom.

Miss Graves says, "Okay, you can play on the concrete, but no keepsies." That's all right 'cause I don't want to lose mine.

Every recess we play marbles. More and more people bring 'em. There're circles all over the place. Winter comes and we can't play outside, so we play on the classroom floors. It's not good. They roll too easy. Spring comes and we go marbling again. I'm getting better and better.

"Hey, everybody, we've only got a week before school's out. Let's play keepsies. We won't tell Miss Graves. Whoever has the most at the end of the week is champion," I suggest.

My friends think it's a great idea. Teachers never come on the playground. They won't know.

Winners of their circle on Monday play each other on Tuesday. Tuesday's winners play on Wednesday and so on until Friday there's only me and Bobby. There's been some tears and some angry kids, but no one tattles.

We count our marbles. He has three more than I do. Oh, this is gonna be a challenge. We each put in six marbles. He knocks one of mine out right off the bat. I tick one of his and my shooter stays in the middle. Oh, no. He's gonna shoot me out and win. I hold my breath. He hits it, but it doesn't go out. Now I get to shoot one of his. One thing is, you have to know your own marbles real well cause you don't want to shoot your own out.

I shoot hard. It hits one of mine, but mine hits one of his and out it goes. "Yeah!" the kids yell. We go at it neck and neck, as Daddy would say. We both only have one left in the ring. Who's gonna win?

"What in the world's going on out here?" I look up. It's Miss Graves.

"Um, Bobby and I are p-playing for the ch-championship," I stutter.

"By the looks of your bag, I'd say you're playing for keeps," she accuses.

"No, Ma'am," Bobby lies. "We're just keeping count of marbles."

Not one of our friends says a word. Bobby and I pick up our own marble and walk into school with a smirk on our faces. We are the champions.

* * *

It's April, and I make my daily rounds of our property with Lassie. We've done this since I brought her home. While we walk, I tell her about my day, my dreams, my writing, my music. She listens and stays right with me. She's a good dog.

Today, I'm upset. When I got home, Mama and Daddy told me they sold our land on the alley to some people named Carl and Bonnie Eller.

"They sold part of the pasture and alfalfa, Lassie," I complain. "That cuts off the trail we go down to visit the Snyders. Why would they do that? We won't be able to go on that land again. They're making our walk shorter." I go on and on and by the time I get back to the house, I feel better. I'd never gripe at my parents. They know what's best, but I certainly don't understand.

On Saturday, Daddy and I go to the lumberyard in our old green pickup. He calls it his International. "She's a good old truck." He pats the steering wheel. "Hauls hay, calves, pigs. Takes meat ta the locker and sacks of feed fur animals. Now, she's gonna haul lumber, cement, and nails."

I look at him with a question mark on my face. "We're gonna' build something?"

"Gonna add onta the house." he says with a satisfied smile. "You're gettin' bigger and need 'en a room of your own. We're plannin' on makin' a new living room and a bedroom for us. You get the old livin' room for your bedroom; make a big closet in it, then put a bathroom tween the bedrooms. How's that sound?"

We bump along. I'm speechless. I realize this is why they sold the land. It's why Mama and Daddy had so many late-night talks after I went to bed. They're using the money from the land to make our house bigger. I'm sorry I was griping.

I finally find my voice. "Can I help?"

"We're plannin' on it." he replies.

Chapter 31

BIGGEST EVER CHASE REUNION

Sharon

A humongous (I just learned that word) event is happening in our family. It's July 4th, and we're headed to Uncle John and Aunt Purna's ranch. Everybody is—that's if they're a Chase. It's a Chase reunion. Lots of people will be there. Chases had big families in my daddy's time as a kid. There were four boys and three girls in his family. In my grandpa Chase's family, there were four boys: Charlie, John, Albert and George. They all had big families. Now they've all got kids and grandkids. We're getting together for a reunion. Oh, yes. It's going to be the biggest get together ever.

"Only two more hills and a turn and we'll be there. Oh, look, there's cars parked all the way out here." I shout. I have eighteen cousins. Mama says I have scads of second and third cousins too. "Look at all the people. They're all over from Uncle John's house down to the old schoolhouse by the creek."

"I see Clifford," I shout. I roll down the window. "Hi, Clifford!" I yell. He waves and comes running to our car as Daddy finds a place to park. Clifford's almost my age and my best Chase cousin.

I jump out and meet him. "Wow. Did ya ever guess we're part of all these people?"

"I've already met five cousins our age. Come on, I'll show you." He grabs my hand and pulls me toward the playground where the merry-go-round can't even be seen 'cause there's so many kids on it. "Hey guys, this is Sharon. My cousin," he hollers.

"Hi, Sharon." they all say at once. "I'm your cousin . . ."

It's a jumble of names, and we laugh. They make room for us and a couple of bigger cousins begin to push. It's heavy; hard to get going. Maybe I won't get sick if we go this slow. After three times around, I jump off 'cause my stomach is doing flip-flops. I sit at a picnic table by a couple of girls to let it settle.

"I'm Georgia," says the girl with long brown pigtails. "I belong to Grandpa George's family. This is Becky. She's my sister—two years younger."

"I'm Sharon. I belong to Tom," I say. I've never thought of me that way before and giggle. "I live in the Lewiston Orchards. Where do you live?"

"You've never been there. Our father doesn't allow visitors," Georgia explains. "We live up the Selway River on the other side of the river from the road. That old red truck over there is ours. We park on the side of the road where we keep our horses. To get to our house, we go across the river in a basket that's hung on a rope. We have to pull on the rope to move the wheels on both ends. It makes the basket move to the other side."

"Really? How do you get to school?" I ask.

"We don't go to public school," Becky replies. "Mother says they don't teach properly. She's our teacher until we turn fifteen, then we'll basket across the river and ride the horse into town where there's a high school."

"Really?" I say again. I can't think of anything else to say to these two girls who have very proper language.

"Our father says that the world is a mess and he doesn't want us influenced by the wrong people. This is the first time we've been allowed to meet other Chase family members," Georgia explains. "Since you're family, I think he would allow you to come visit."

"He would have to ask my father," I say, very aware of how I'm pronouncing my words.

"Of course." Becky nods. "We'll ask him to send you a formal invitation."

Oh, my, I'm thinking. The Selway River? We went fishing there once when I was seven. It's a steep river, rushing out of the mountain with big boulders and white water splashing up. I've had some horrible water experiences. Going across there in a basket sounds like a nightmare.

The old school bell rings. Everyone gathers at the front door. It becomes quiet. Adults bow their heads and Uncle John says grace. Me too. It seems like both Mama and Daddy's family always thank God for the food when we're with them. We never do that at home. I see Mama and slip through the people to stand with her. The line is long, long, long. I hope there'll be food left by the time we get in there.

It's finally our turn in the door. I didn't need to worry. The school house has sawhorse tables all the way around the room with loads of food. Every family brought double enough for their own. The problem is choosing. My plate is heaped by the time I get around the room.

Mama says, "You can eat with the kids on the bank down by the creek if you want to. Just don't go wandering off too far so we can find you when we want to leave."

I walk carefully, trying not to spill. Desserts were on the last table. I put my cookies on top of all my other food. I'll have to eat my dessert first. Yum.

I look for Georgia and Becky, thinking I'd like to sit with them. I spy them at the same picnic table sitting properly with their three brothers and mother and father. I balance my plate and walk slowly down to the creek and sit by Clifford and David.

It's good we're on a ranch. No neighbors to complain about the noise: people laughing, talking, kids yelling and screaming, babies crying. What a commotion! Mama says there's two hundred and nine Chases here. I wonder if we'll ever see each other again.

Chapter 32

1950

BACK TO THE ORCHARDS

Sharon

This summer new neighbors move into Janice and Shirley's house. The mama's name is Marie and her girl is Phyllis. Mama and I visit and welcome them to the neighborhood. I know we're going to be friends right off the bat. Phyllis likes to ride her bike.

She can't walk or run like I do. Mama says she was born crippled. Boy, can she ride her bike fast. We ride up and down Grelle. There's a hill down by Leachman's. It takes lots of muscle to get to the top. It's sure fun coming down. I love how the wind blows in my face.

When they start harvesting peas on the farms at the end of Grelle, we have to listen or rather smell a pea truck coming, pull over to the side of the road and stop. Those guys really truck it down the road. I think the drivers want to get to the dumping place as quick as they can. The silage from the vines where the big machines cuts them gets rotten real fast when it's hot. Yuk! What a stink. You can smell it in our house.

The Adams start going to the Orchard's Community Church on the bus with Mama and me. They don't have a car. Mrs. Adams starts a club for neighborhood kids at her house. It's called LTL. That stands for Loyal Temperance Legion. It means we learn all about alcohol and how we should never drink any, cause it isn't good for our body. We sing songs, play games and work on papers so we can get a badge.

There's forty-four kids in our block. Only eight to twelve- year-old's are in the club.

Phyllis is a year older than me. We're good friends. We both like to sing. Her mama plays the piano and we sing along. I love it.

*　　*　　*

Houses aren't built quick. It's been four months and we only have the foundation poured on the new part of our house. Daddy only works on it on his days off. His two weeks off at the railroad, he drives the grain truck. Mama and I don't know his plan, so we can only do a few things like keep things clean and organized. I see right now it won't be done till next summer. It's like Mama says, "Good things take a long time to cook."

School starts. I go back to The Orchards School in fifth grade. That means I move up to the second floor. Many of my fifth-grade friends aren't here anymore. They go to the new school in the other end of the Orchards. It's called Warner School. Even my friend Judy has to go there. Seems like it didn't do much good 'cause my classroom is in a corner of the auditorium. Are there still too many kids for the classrooms?

I know most of the thirty-five kids in class, but there are some new ones. A girl named Ardie and I become good friends. Her dad's the pastor of the Advent Christian Church where Mama and I go on Sunday night with our neighbor's, the Jensens or Snyders.

Our teacher is Miss Satre. She's short, beautiful, and isn't married. She has a boyfriend named Tony who is way too tall. Bobby and Lonnie tease her. "Hey, Miss Satre, do you stand on a chair or get a ladder to kiss Tony?" She smiles and blushes.

"Class, today you're getting new books," our teacher announces. "We need to take extra good care of them. Classes will use them for the next few years. This book is about the United States of America. We're going to find out how big our country is, how the government is formed, and who the important people were that set up the rules we live by."

I'm impatient to get my hands on that book. She writes the name of each student and the book number as she calls out names. I hurry back to my seat, open it and read the first chapter by the time the last book's given out. My mind keeps saying, I didn't know that. That really happened? How come no one ever told me this?

There's another thing I love about this class. It has a library. There's at least a hundred books in the shelves under the windows. I want to read them all. I hurry through my work so I can read.

The school has a hot lunch program now. The community people provide most of the food. There're two cooks who make lunch in the attic. We climb a one-person wide stair, get our tray of food, and sit at long tables with benches. There's not even a window. I watch the cooks and wonder, what would happen to us if there was a fire? This is scary. Hot lunch is ten cents. I mostly bring my lunch. Even if we bring our lunch, we eat up there. Like other years, Mama makes sandwiches out of ground meat mixed with cream and puts it in my lunch pail along with vegetables and fruit. Sometimes toward spring, we don't have much meat in the locker, so I get bacon-grease sandwiches. That's OK. I like them.

They're making a new building beside the school. It's going to be our new place to eat. They call it a cafeteria. It's supposed to be done before winter.

The furnace often goes out in the school. They let us wear coats, hats and gloves, and even boots if we have them. It's still hard to concentrate on work. Frost forms on the inside of the windows. We cheer when the pipes begin to clang. The heaters warm the room enough to melt the window frost, then the furnace quits, and it turns to ice. It gets thicker and thicker. We measure it for math.

I'm ten years old and Mama still makes me wear those long, brown, cotton stockings held up by a garter belt. They're ugly and embarrassing. When we get to school, I unhook them and roll them down just above my shoes. Ah, the freedom. It doesn't matter how cold it is or that my dress gives little protection. It's my big rebellion.

"Class, today we're going to have a special treat. Mr. Williams is coming with a projector to show a moving picture." Miss Satre sounds excited. "The whole school's coming to the auditorium to see a story called, Ricki Tikki Tavi. It's about a boy in India, who owns a pet mongoose. When a snake threatens the boy, the mongoose saves him. We'll talk about it afterward."

Students come and sit in rows on the floor. We turn our desks around and sit. That's when we notice the big white screen up by the stage and a black machine with big wheels sitting on a table.

The story has a real boy, a real snake, and a real mongoose. I've never heard of that animal before. I've never seen a movie with real people and animals either. When I was seven, Aunt Edna took Patty and me to see Snow White and the Seven Dwarfs. They were just drawings. Even if it wasn't real, that movie scared me to death.

*   *   *

It's almost Christmas. I love this time of year. Our fifth and sixth-grade choir has practiced for a month. Miss Satre's voice sings beautifully as she plays the piano. She teaches us to sing like we play in the band—loud and soft, high and low, fast and slow.

The whole school's doing a Christmas concert. I have a solo in Silent Night and sing a verse with Ardie and Pauline in Jolly Ol' Saint Nicholas. Between the band and choir, I perform in nine songs. I'd sing all day if they let me.

If that's not exciting enough, they opened the new cafeteria yesterday. It's got big windows all the way around. At one end you can see the kitchen. It's beyond the counter where the trays are stacked. Mrs Day and Mrs Cook stand smiling. I bet they're happy to have this place. I get to eat hot lunch two days in a row. Mmm. I love their spinach as long as they let me put vinegar and salt on it. Other kids don't like it and give theirs to me. I'm in spinach heaven. Today, we had my favorite meal: mashed potatoes with hamburger gravy. I'm thinking no more bacon grease sandwiches.

We didn't have a tree at Old Webster last year. There's always a huge Christmas tree in the main hall for the whole month of December at Orchards. Every class makes decorations to put on it. The tree will have a sack for each of us the last day before vacation. It will hold an orange, nuts and candy.

Mr. Haynes, our new principal, brings all the students around the tree every morning to say the Pledge of Allegiance, sing America, and have Bible reading and prayer. Then he has two classes choose a Christmas carol to sing before we go to class.

*   *   *

One of those Christmas carols says: "Christmas Eve is coming, and the goose is getting fat . . ." Well, let me tell you about a Christmas goose.

Grandma's getting too old to cook Christmas dinner, so we're going to Aunt Edna's. On Saturday, she calls my mom.

"We're going to have goose for Christmas dinner. We'll kill it tomorrow. Can Sharon come help Patty pluck it so I can put it in salt water overnight? Around two o'clock?"

Pluck a goose? I've plucked chickens all my life, but never a goose. They're much bigger. Sure, I'll help do that. I put on some old clothes. When I get to Aunt Edna's, Patty takes me to their back screened porch. There's a galvanized bath tub with the carcass lying in it. Aunt Edna pours boiling hot water over it to make the feathers come loose and we start pulling.

Big feathers are easy. But under the big feathers are a gazillion little feathers that fly around the room like snow and get in our hair, our eyes, up our nose. We sneeze and sneeze. We're supposed to keep the little feathers in an old pillowcase to be made into a pillow. Impossible. They not only fly, they stick to our wet hands. Hot water and feathers stink. Usually, plucking's done outside. It's snowy and cold, so we're trapped with the putrid smell. Let me tell you, I gag more than once.

Five hours later, Patty and I finish. Aunt Edna finishes the few we miss and Daddy picks me up. This is the worst idea for Christmas dinner, ever. Even when the goose is roasting in the oven on Christmas Day, it smells like wet feathers. I can't eat a bite.

All those little feathers we tried to get into the pillowcase? Well, there's not enough for a mouse's pillow. They'll have to eat a lot more geese. Believe me, I won't be plucking them.

*   *   *

The first week of April. I get off the bus and start walking toward home. I feel something hit my back. I turn quick and see Lonnie, who lives three houses from the corner, picking up more rocks.

"What are you doing?" I yell. He throws another at me. Then another. I turn and run home. He's laughing.

This happens the next day and the next and the next. Finally, I can't stand it.

"Stop it," I yell at him. He keeps aiming for me.

"Mama," I yell as I throw open the door. "You told me to never tattle, but I can't take it anymore." By this time, I'm in tears.

"Honey, what's wrong?" Mama puts her arm around me and we sit on the davenport. "Tell me."

"Lonnie won't quite throwing rocks at me," I say between sobs.

"What? Why would he do that? Did you do something to upset him?" She asks.

"I don't think so. I hardly ever talk to him. I can't think why he's being so mean."

I'm beginning to get my breath. "I don't know what to do. He's been doing it for a week."

"Let's go talk to his mom. I bet Ann doesn't know." We walk back down the street toward White's house. His mother, Ann, is the daughter of my favorite neighbors, the Yarbers. That makes Lonnie their real grandson. They built a house on Yarber's land next to Grandma and Grandpa.

Ann's surprised to see us. I see Lonnie run down the hall and hide. Mama explains why we're here.

"Lonnie, come here," Ann yells. He comes down the hall with his head down and doesn't even look at us. "Why in the world are you throwing rocks at Sharon? She's a nice girl. You don't treat her like that." He mumbles something. "I can't hear you, Lonnie. Look at me and tell me."

Slowly he raises his head and looks at his Mama. "I do it because I like her," he finally says.

Silence—then I hear my Mama clear her throat. I can hear a smile in her voice, but it's not on her face.

"Lonnie, when you like someone, you're good to them and you do nice things for them. Throwing rocks at someone doesn't make them like you."

"Sorry," Lonnie mutters. Then he looks at me. "Will you sit by me on the bus on Monday?" I don't know how to answer. Mama squeezes my hand and I say, "OK."

Chapter 33

SIXTH GRADE

Sharon

It's funny how things work sometimes. I was expecting to be in a classroom this year, but no, they switched classes and put the fifth graders in a room and our sixth grade is at the back ofthe auditorium. The teacher's different though.

He introduces himself. "I'm Mr. Carroll Johnson. This year will be demanding. I will be preparing you to go to Junior High. You'll not just be learning subjects, you'll learn how to learn."

A man teacher? I've only had Mr. Woods for band one hour a week and he gets grouchy sometimes. I'm a little afraid of Mr. Johnson. He has a paddle lying on his desk. He's tall, with black wavy hair and piercing blue eyes that look down a long nose. He is handsome, I think.

"Get out your notebooks," he demands on the first day. "On the first page you're going to write the rules of our class."

I promptly follow directions and have my pencil ready to write. I hear Greta and Molly talking and giggling in the outside row. Whack! The paddle comes down on the desk. We jump and freeze with eyes on the teacher.

"Rule number one: Talking to another student during class is not allowed. Write it on the first line." The room is silent as a funeral parlor without the organ playing. The only sound is pencils scratching across the paper. I glance at Greta and Molly. They silently laugh holding their hands over their mouths. In two strides, Mr. Johnson is by Greta's desk, grabs her arm and takes her in the hall where we hang our coats. "Whack." We hear the paddle. A red-faced Greta returns and sits quietly. Mr. Johnson enters and sits at his desk. His face is red too. We all get the point.

*   *   *

Mr. Johnson's reading Uncle Tom's Cabin out loud in class. The story raises hundreds of questions. At first, I think it takes place in some other country. He makes it clear it's a story about people living in the southern part of the United States. Really? It has people with black skin who don't talk the same as us.

I've never met anyone, except Mr. Blue, who has black skin. Mr. Blue lives on Snake River Ave. close to where the circus sets up their tents. He's called Blue Pete by most people. His real name is Milton H. Davis. He got his nickname from telling someone to bet on a horse named Blue Pete—it won. He and his black and white dog come to the grocery store downtown. The dog pulls a wagon to carry stuff home he buys. That's pretty smart. It's a long way to his house. He's always stops to talk with me. I like his smile and the twinkle in his eyes.

Are there other black people who live in the United States? Mama and I go to the Orchard's Community Church. A man named John Newman, who's a missionary in Africa, shows pictures of people where he lives. They have black skin. That's why I think the book happens there. I can tell I don't know much about my country.

Mr. Johnson finishes the book and gives us an assignment— actually it's homework. I've never had homework before. "Your assignment is to write a factual story about the days of slavery in the United States. It can be about one person, a family or events. You'll need to go to the library to find your information."

The library? I've read all the books in our library and there's nothing about slaves. I bravely stay after class to ask about the library.

"It's downtown in Pioneer Park," he explains.

"Really?" Amazing! I run to catch my bus.

There's no one else on the bus to get off at my stop, so Mr. Utz drops me in front of my house.

I run in the house shouting, "Mama, did you know there's a library downtown?"

"I heard they had one, but I've never been there," she replies. "I thought since we don't live in Lewiston, we can't use it."

"No, no! We can. Mr. Johnson gave us homework and told us we can find books about it at the library in Pioneer Park." I shout. "Can we go now?"

"It's too late today. By the time we take the bus, the library will be closed. Tomorrow's Saturday. Let's go then." Mama always has a way of knowing how to plan. I have to wait until tomorrow. Life sure has a lot of waiting.

*　　*　　*

There's rows and rows and rooms and rooms of books at this library. How in the world will I find what I'm looking for?

"Let's ask the lady at the desk," Mama suggests. "Excuse me," she begins, "My daughter and I have never been in a library before. She has a homework assignment and needs help finding the subject."

I see the lady's eyes go wide like she can't believe we're real. She looks at me, finds her voice and asks, "What subject are you looking for?"

"I need to read about real people who lived as slaves in the South." I explain.

"Ah, come with me," she directs as she walks to the back of the library and into another room. "Do you have a library card? Well, of course you don't if you've never been in a library. We'll fill out one so you can take three books home. They have to be back to the library in two weeks. Here you are. You'll find your informational books on these three shelves."

Three shelves? How long do I have to look at all those books? Mama and I start reading the content pages and first chapters. So much, so much. We find three and take them back to the desk. The lady's ready for me to sign a card. I proudly walk out with three books. My report will be about Booker T. Washington. He was born into a slave family. After they were freed, he started a school for people like himself. I discover from a newspaper report that Blue Pete went to his school. Isn't that great?

* * *

There's a new boy in our class named Cody. He's tall, blond, with light colored eyes. He seems to like me. I think I could like him, too. He's been calling me on the phone after school.

On Saturday he calls. "Are you going to be home? I want to come visit."

"Just a minute," I say. I ask Mama, "Are we going to be home today? Cody wants to come visit."

"We're not going to town today. Daddy's working," Mama nods and smiles.

"We'll be here." I reply in my best controlled voice.

Cody responds, "Good, I'll be there in about an hour."

I hang up thinking, Oh my. A boy's coming to see me. Not a neighbor boy—a real boy. What will we do? What will I say? My heart's thumping. I forget to breathe.

"He'll be here in an hour." I inform Mama.

"An hour?" Mama questions. "Good. That will give us time to bake some oatmeal cookies."

Mama's keeping me busy. I think she knows I'm nervous. As I take the last cookies out of the oven there's a knock on the door. It's him!

I walk—no, skip—to the door. I look around the living room. I'm glad we finished the addition to the house last fall. Now we have a proper living room, and most of all, a proper bathroom so company doesn't have to use the outhouse. We live in a modern house. I open the door. There he stands.

"Hi, Cody. 'Come into my parlor, said the spider to the fly.'" I grin. We've just finished reading that poem in school.

"Do I dare?" he laughs. "Mmm, smells good in here."

"Come in the kitchen," I invite. "That's where it smells even better. I might even let you have a taste of the smell."

When we added to the house, we moved the table from the kitchen to the screened in porch and put glass where the screen used to be. Mama already has a big plate of cookies on the table and some cocoa.

"Help yourself," I motion, very aware of how unladylike I plop myself in the chair next to him. Cody dives in. The only sounds are Mama washing up baking pans and the soft chewing of cookies. I finally break the silence. "How'd you get here? I didn't hear a car."

"I walked." He answers between bites. "It's farther than I thought."

"Where do you live?" I ask, wondering how he found out where I live.

"Twelfth and Grelle."

"Eight blocks," I exclaim. "Blocks in the Orchards are a fourth mile? You walked two miles to get here? I'm impressed."

Cody grins. "Yah, but it was worth it." Three chews and a swallow: "These cookies are delicious."

I laugh. Silence again sets in as we eat. I trace the flowers on the table's oilcloth with my little finger, glancing at him, wondering why in the world he would walk two miles here and two miles home.

He gulps down the last of the hot chocolate, takes off his silver "Cody" ID bracelet and hands it to me.

I'm flabbergasted. "I don't know what to say. I . . .I'm . . . I'm surprised. Are you sure you want me to have this?"

"I'm sure. I want you to be my girl and wear it the rest of the year?" He draws in a big breath.

"I need to think about this. I know we're good friends, but this is kind of serious."

"Okay, think about it." He polishes off the last cookie gently, takes my hand, and . . . shakes it. "I've got to head back home so I can get there in time for supper. Mom always expects us on time for meals." He gets up and heads for the door.

"See you Monday, then." I clutch the bracelet, still feeling the warmth of his handshake. "I'll . . .I'll let you know first recess."

Now what am I going to do? I certainly can't tell Mama . . . er . . . Mom (I've noticed my friends call their mothers, Mom. It's more grown up. Mama still calls her parents Mama and Papa though). Anyway, she'd be shocked if she knew what I have in my hand. I'm sure nothing like this ever happened to her.

On Monday. I put on the bracelet, pull my sweater sleeve over it and wear it to school. I'll have to wear long sleeves the rest of the school year.

Little did we know, it would be our 20th class reunion, before the bracelet would find its way back to its original owner.

*   *   *

House with addition

We have Christmas with Mom's side of the family at our house this year. Grandma's not feeling well. She's seventy-seven and deserves not to do a big dinner. Everyone brings something. Aunt Edna, the professional cook of the family, brings a new sweet potato dish. It's made with marshmallows on top. Mmm, is it sweet and yummy. It's the first year of being in our new addition of the house. Look at all the room for people.

It's a calm day. Uncle Johnny and Aunt Alice live in Spokane now and aren't here. Sad to say, that's the reason it's a calm, relaxing day. Aunt Alice always starts picking on someone and then there's a row.

Patty and I go in my room and draw after dinner. My cousin's a great artist. I learn so much from her. When she colors with crayons, she rubs the paper with her finger until the coloring looks like it's been painted.

It's getting late and we all take one last bit of pie and read the Christmas story before everyone goes. They leave leftovers for us to enjoy. I love how we celebrate each other. We give gifts, but they're small, thoughtful, and personal.

*   *   *

Five days later, Mom gets sick. Oh my, is she sick. Vomiting all day since lunch. All night, no sleep. Thank goodness for a toilet; I don't think she'd make it to the outhouse. The next day I call Dr. Stover, the new railroad doctor. He comes to the house. Mom's still not able to eat or drink.

"How soon after lunch did you start throwing up?" He asks.

"About a half hour."

"What did you have to eat?" he questions.

"Leftovers from Christmas. I finished up the ham, potato salad, and the candied sweet potatoes." Mom says in barely a whisper.

"Ah," he replies. "You're the fifth person I've seen the last two days who had left over candied sweet potatoes. You've got food poisoning. Sharon, would you make your mama some strong black tea? Do you have soda crackers in the house?"

I nod and leave to put water on our electric stove and retrieve the crackers from our new metal cabinets.

"Susan, I want you to only have soda crackers and strong black tea for the next two days. That will settle your stomach and get your digestive system back to normal." He gives her some bromide to drink, packs up and leaves. Mom goes to sleep after one cracker and a half cup of tea. Guess I'm going to take care of Mom and the house for a few days.

*   *   *

It snows a lot this winter. We play Fox and Geese in the schoolyard and make snowmen. There's no snowballs allowed. However, down below the school where we play baseball, it's called "no man's land." Everyone, including teachers, can build forts and have snowball fights there.

Today, I'm feeling brave. My friends and I build a big fort to hide behind. We're fighting two different gangs. I only get hit twice. We're pretty good for girls.

The bell rings and everyone has to stop. I have a perfectly good snowball in my mittens right now and I certainly can't waste it. Ted White's the last boy to leave. I heave my missile at him and hit him right in the nose. Blood flies everywhere.

"Ted, I'm sorry, I'm so sorry, I didn't think . . . Oh dear . . . stop, stop, let me put snow on it. It'll stop bleeding." I'm frantically trying to calm him down. His nose is swelling and I can tell his eye is going to be black. "Here, let me put this on your face," I hold a mitten of snow on it.

Slowly the bleeding stops. There's a big patch of red snow in the middle of "no man's land." He calms and we start walking toward the school.

Everyone's gone in. "I'm gonna' be in big trouble, aren't I? I'm sorry, Ted. I feel so bad."

Ted stops, looks at me and smiles. "That was a powerful throw for a girl. Great hit."

When we get to class, Mr. Johnson looks at Ted then me and never says a word.

* * *

Mr. Johnson and Miss Satre's classes are doing a play called, "Polly Make Believe." We try out for parts. I get the part of Lassie. I'm one of the kids who travel to different parts of the United States where people settled from other countries. My grandpa's family came from Holland. I love the song they sing:

Oh, we are from Holland and and we are Dutch, Dutch
And we like American Country much, much

We'll make of you cheeses and all of such, such.
Oh, won't you be happy mit us.

Everyone sings the songs. I have speaking parts. We'll perform it for our families in March. Wow! Do I ever love being in plays.

I wonder if I'll ever travel the world, see these countries we sing about, meet the people. I have a pen-pal from Germany in class this year. We send letters back and forth. Her name is Adelheid Schleicher. She lives in a house close to the Aa Lake. Her school was destroyed in the war, so they go to classes in at the Munster Hansalatz in Handelslehranstalten while their school's being rebuilt. She tells me stories about many buildings destroyed in war. How terrifying it must have been to live there during bombs. I remember how frightened I was with planes flying over. At her house, they didn't just fly over, they dropped bombs. How scared she must have been.

She sends me pictures. Her English is very good. She also sends me the old German way of writing the alphabet and writes a letter using it. It's like a puzzle trying to read it. It takes three days to rewrite it in regular alphabet. I like the old way they make some letters, especially the r. I practice and practice until I can write my name using that r. Wouldn't it be fun if I could go visit her.

*　　*　　*

Remember how Mama had to tie cheese cloth around our faucet in spring to filter out the mud, fish and frogs? Well, that won't happen anymore. The Lewiston Orchards has it's very own water filtering plant. Mr. Johnson's and Miss Satre's classes make a bus trip out there. It's a big, yellow, brick building in the middle of a wheat field, about two miles from where I live. It seems complicated with pipes, on and off valves and levers.

The man who gives us the tour says, "You'll never have to pick another frog out of your glass of water." We all laugh.

*　　*　　*

Mama keeps our house spic and span clean. She's moving furniture, mopping, and dusting. It's not even cleaning day—that's on Thursdays.

"Goodness, Mom. Are you expecting company?" I look up from the desk where I'm writing my final report on the state of Idaho.

"You never know when someone's going to pop in. I always want our house to look good."

"Do you want me to help? At least I'll move my desk." I pull my new, wooden desk to the middle of the room.

She smiles, shakes her head and mops there. "You just get your homework finished. I'm doing fine."

I don't know where she gets all her energy. She washes clothes all morning and hangs them on the line because it's Monday. Now she's mopping floors.

I turn in my report the next day. Whew. Glad that's done. I learned a lot. The capital is Boise, but it used to be Lewiston. That's strange. The state bird is a Blue Bird, and the state flower is the Syringa. It was the forty-third to become part of the United States on July 3, 1890. Goodness, my Grandma was sixteen years old then. We had a test on Idaho facts today. I got 100.

I jump off the bus and run home to tell Mom, throw open the door and stand speechless. Against the inside wall of the living room, there's a … piano. A huge piano. It takes up half the wall.

I let out a scream. "A piano? A real piano?" Mom, Dad, neighbors, aunts and uncles pour through the kitchen door.

"Surprise, surprise!" they yell.

"I … I … I don't understand. It's not even my birthday," I gasp.

"Nope," Dad says. "We want ya ta have it before school's out so's ya can take lessons this summer."

I'm squealing, crying and shaking. I've dreamed of playing the piano ever since I heard one at church. I sit down on the round stool and plunk out Mary Had a Little Lamb. Everyone claps.

My piano teacher is Mrs Fisher. She lives on Burrell, the next street down from us and close to eighteenth. I ride my bike there. She teaches me how to read notes in the music and match them to the keys on the piano. I know the names of them for the right hand from band. That's the treble cleft. The left hand doesn't listen to my brain as well.

The bass cleft is hard. I practice and practice. She says I'm a natural. A natural what I don't know. By the end of summer, she's teaching me chords and how to put them with the right-hand melody. I spend every extra minute playing that piano. I love it. Daddy, I mean Dad, says they can afford only one year of lessons. I'll be really good in one year.

*   *   *

It's the last day of school; the opposite end of first grade. The last time I'll say the pledge, pray, have Bible reading, play with my friends from the last six years. I'm sad and scared. Orchard's School is my second home. Good times here. Memories galore. I know we'll be going to the same Junior High. So will all the sixth graders in Lewiston. I'm a country bumpkin going to the big city school. Am I ready? Will they like me? Am I smart enough? Cody still comes every Saturday. I'm still wearing his bracelet. Will that change in Junior High? Guess I'll find out next fall.

Chapter 34

1952

IT HAPPENED!

Susan

Our daughter's childhood passed like one short sleep. At five foot six, she's a brown-eyed Chase who possesses confidence and tackles new experiences with great gusto. All else fades as I'm captivated by her boldness, her voice, her talents. She's grown beyond my capabilities. She's crossed my bridge of trust, listened and accepted God's wisdom, developed a cheerful, kind heart and chosen to follow Jesus. Discipline and independence replace me. I can only supply support beams with each stone she lays in her own bridge. Isn't that the role of a bridge? Get someone to the other side? Help them continue their journey?

Sharon will head ten miles down the hill to Junior High next fall. What have I missed in her childhood? Could I have done more? Did I do too much? Questions plague me. No rock solid answers come. It doesn't matter. That time's come and gone. It can't be changed.

The ache in my heart is for Tom. How happy he'd be if he listened to God. He's missed experiences with his daughter. They've been close but not tied together in faith like she and I are.

"Daddy, please come to church with us this morning," Sharon pleads. "Nope," Tom answers.

When we come home, she sits on the footstool in front of his chair and tells him the Bible story and verse she learned. He sits silent, reading his newspaper.

"Isn't that a great story?" she asks. He continues reading his newspaper.

His non-response makes her more determined.

A "yes" to the question of church comes only when Sharon's going to do something—sing, play, recite, tell a story. He's proud of his little girl who's changing into a young lady. What will happen to their relationship?

Summer's when Tom and Sharon work together. Alfalfa's cut, shocked, dried and hauled into the barn every two weeks. The garden's cultivated and rows weeded. Baby animals need care. They make a good team. I've no idea what they talk about out there.

"God," I entreat. "Put yourself in the middle of their conversations. I trust you to take care of my Tom. I want him to be full of your joy."

* * *

Sharon

I live in a triangle: home, school, church. The school corner's empty, open, unknown. I want to learn. Do more. See more. Know more. Exciting. Scary.

I have to say, I'm one lucky girl to have my mom and dad, grandparents, aunts, uncles and neighbors. I don't know a single person who doesn't like me. Other kids tell me it's not alway like that.

If I could change one thing, I'd want Dad to know Jesus like I do. He's a good father. He loves me and wants the best for me, but he won't even talk about God. He ignores me when I talk "religious stuff," as he calls it. Or he gives me a gruff "Hurumph!" Mama says I've got to leave Dad up to God. If I'm going to do that, I'll have to talk to God a lot.

Chapter 35

First Job Failure

Sharon

I love, love, love summer. Love the heat, love things growing, love baby animals. I go to Grandma and Grandpa Kole's in June to pick black caps and raspberries. Grandpa pays five cents a Hallock now. I got a raise 'cause I pick faster. I want new clothes for school, so I'm saving every bit of my berry money. Town kids dress different. I've been a hick from the sticks all my life. If I'm going to fit in down there, I need "in" clothes. No more homemade or cheapy dresses. At the end of berry season, I have twenty-two dollars.

"Hi, older than me cousin," I say when Patty answers the phone. "Would you go clothes shopping with me before school starts?" She's going into tenth grade. She knows what's "in."

"Sure, we'll go the second week of August when the stores get fall clothes. If you really want the "in" clothes they have to be Jantzen," she tells me. "How much have you saved?"

"Twenty-two dollars," I proudly say.

There's silence on the other end. "Patty?" I ask.

"Uh . . . OK," she finally responds. "If you want to buy the "in" stuff you'll need more than that. Like at least fifty dollars."

Oh, dear. I need to find another job. "Oh, I will" I try to sound confident. "Thanks." I hang up defeated. Whew! Where will I get that kind of money. Town kids must all be rich.

I let friends and family know I need a job. Aunt Edna finds me my first job ironing clothes for a lady. That's funny. The only thing I've ever ironed is hankies and pillowcases.

"Mom, show me how to do the rest," I beg.

"Before you iron, you have to sprinkle the clothes," she instructs. She takes a pop bottle, fills it with water, puts a plug with pin holes in the top and shakes it over a dress. "Don't get it too wet. You just want it damp when it's time to iron." She rolls it up tight and puts it in the pink "ironing" tub that used to be my baby bath tub. "Go ahead and sprinkle the rest. Then we wait at least a half hour."

What am I going to do for a half hour at this lady's house while I'm waiting for the clothes to get damp? I'd better take along a book or maybe a writing tablet.

I set up the wooden ironing board in the kitchen and plug in the iron. Mom still has her old flat iron she used to heat on the wood stove. I'm thankful for this electric one we got with our green stamps. I bet Mom is too.

She shows me how to fold Dad's pants and iron a crease down them then put them over the end and do the upper part. Same with shirts: iron one side of the front, the other front, back, collar and then make the sleeves with creases down the outside. Dresses go over the end of the board. You iron the top half, then the skirt, pulling it over the end and around the ironing board. They're easier. Yes, I can do this.

On Monday, Aunt Edna drives me to Mrs. Shane's house downtown, introduces us and leaves. This lady seems nice. I'm worried about doing a good enough job. The house is big, beautiful and has fancy furniture. She takes me to the ironing room where the board is set up and waiting for me. I look around. There's a basket of clothes, but I don't see a sprinkling bottle or a dampening pan. I go back to the living room where she's reading.

"Excuse me," I use my politest voice. "Can you tell me where to find the sprinkling bottle?"

"Oh, you don't need one," she assures me. "It's a steam iron. Fill it with water. The steam takes the wrinkles out."

I retreat back to my assignment, find the little cup at the end of the board, get water from the bathroom and try to fill the iron. *There must be a secret to this*, I tell myself. *Must be a button or something.* The water wouldn't go in. After three attempts, I go back to the living room.

"I'm sorry, I've never used this kind of iron. Would you show me how to fill it?"

"Of course," she says. "You must be from the Orchards. People who live there can't afford new things." She gets up, fills the iron by pushing the red button and goes back to her reading. I'm glad she leaves immediately so she can't see the embarrassment and anger boiling over in my red face.

The iron begins to huff and puff. Steam pours out holes in the bottom. I take a shirt from the basket, lay in on the board and cautiously place the iron on the shirt. It sputters, spits out water and soaks the front of the shirt. Oh dear, how do I get that dry? I iron over and over and over the wet spot. It keeps spreading.

Near tears, I humbly go back to the living room. "Sorry to disturb you again, but the iron is spitting water. Is it supposed to do that?"

Mrs. Shane throws down her magazine and stomps into the ironing room. "Look," she elevates her voice. "You have it on the wrong setting. It's too hot." She moves the little black lever and stomps back to her reading.

For the next two hours I fight with the iron. It hisses and spits at me. It irons more wrinkles into the clothes than out. It burns me three times with unexpected puffs of steam. Finally the basket's empty.

I call Aunt Edna to pick me up.

"Here's ten dollars for your efforts," Mrs. Shane shoves a bill in my hand. "Ironing's clearly not your best talent." I've failed my first real job.

Chapter 36

NEW NEIGHBORS, NEW FRIENDS

Sharon

Have you ever noticed a few things stay the same, but most things keep changing? Our neighborhood has new houses and new families. Mom, Dad and I go visit when they move in and take food.

Charlie Rosenkrantz moved an enormous, two story farm house onto the vacant land across the road from our raspberry patch. Who would ever think you could move a whole house?

It's funny. Mom knew Charlie when he and his brother were growing up on the prairie. Their family had money. Always bought the latest in everything: first phone, first car, first airplane. Mom said her family didn't fraternize much with them (I think that means being social). Guess the boys were wild kids. She told me stories about them stealing an outhouse and putting it on top of the school along with other "pranks," especially on Halloween.

Now, here's Charlie, his wife and his son Bobby living across from us. We take them a pie. They thank us, take the pie and chat a bit, but never invite us in. Guess they still don't fraternize.

Mrs. Richardson's son built a little house on her property next to Grelle. It only has two bedrooms. They already have three kids and the mom's going to have another. Where in the world are they going to put that baby? They're younger than Mom and Dad. The kids aren't in school yet. We take cookies to them. More kids added to the neighborhood.

On 20th street, a family named Jensen moves into a flat roofed house. They have three girls and a boy. Mom and Gladys become good friends through a Bible study they go to at Marie Adams. Gladys drives. Mom doesn't. So Mom and I go with them to town, to pick strawberries, to Sunday night church at the Advent Christian Church where RD's dad is pastor. Sometimes we just go for a drive in the country. Mom and Gladys have a discussion about which kind of cow is best—a Holstein or a Hereford.

The Jensen's have a huge raspberry patch beside their house. When we walk over there to visit, us kids play hide and seek in the raspberries; great places to hide, plus you can eat while you wait to get found or see your chance to run to safety. It's especially exciting in the dark.

Twenty-four kids. Our block has twenty-four kids. I may be an only child, but our yard is always full of kids. I am never without friends.

Chapter 37

1952

Another Tent meeting

Tom

I just ain't ready for my Pumpkin ta grow up. Feel like I wasted time wishin' for more babies. Finally gave up and worked on being daddy ta Sharon. We done lots: fishin', huckleberryin', hayin', raisin' lambs, growin' food. Even took us ta Portland to visit Sister Frankie and ta Spokane to see Susie's Aunt Grace and Uncle Archie. Done lots more than my father did with me.

My favorite time's when she'd goes with me in the ol' International pickup ta the Lewiston Roller Mills ta get hog feed or oats for the cow. The half hour trip down and half hour back gives lots a time ta talk 'bout things. She's such a smart youngin'. Smarter than I'll ever be seein' as how I had no learnin' after third grade.

Sometimes she asks 'bout things I never heard of. Like Pampas Plains in Argen . . . oh, cain't remember the country now, in South America. She reads 'bout places like that. Says they got cowboys. Didn't know that.

I learn from her. She teaches me the right way ta say things. I'm tryin' hard ta remember. One word she says embarrasses her is "ain't". Workin' ta get that outa my language so she'll be proud of me.

One thing I cain't make myself do is say yes ta her askin' me ta church. She talks 'bout Jesus like he's a friend. Don't see how that's

167

right. When I's a kid in church, I heard he's perfect. I never can be perfect so he's not wantin' to hang 'round me. People in the church ain't—I mean aren't— perfect, so I call 'em hypocrites. Got nuthin' in common, 'cause I know I'm not perfect.

"Dad, will you come to the Hyman Appleman meetings with Mama and me? Sharon asks me taday.

"Who's he?" I question. "That's some kind of strange name."

"I don't know," she replies, "He's talking in a big white tent on Lewiston's Main Street in that empty lot where the funeral parlor used to be. Mom and I are going with Aunt Neen."

"Not a church?"

"No, just a tent with benches."

"Time?"

"Neen said to be ready by six-thirty on Friday night."

"Humph!" is the only response I can think of. If'n it's not a church, I don't have no excuse. Curious 'bout a man with a strange name who talks in tents. Been to camp meetings. Not bad. Singin's good. I'll think 'bout this.

*   *   *

Susan

It's Friday. Sharon and I sit in our living room waiting for Tom's sister to pick us up. I don't know where Tom is. He hides when he thinks he's going to be pressured into something God related.

There's a crunch of gravel. "Ah, there's Neen. Let's go, Sharon." As we start out the door, I hear heavy footsteps and turn around. It's Tom. He's cleaned up, has on his best shirt and his hair slicked back. I start to say something, then shut my mouth, afraid he'll change his mind.

Neen must feel the same way. Her eyes sparkle and she smiles, but doesn't say a word until we're down the road a piece.

"Sure am glad I cleaned the car inside and out today," she comments. "It's not often I get to have a full load. This is fun." She glances sideways at Tom in the front passenger seat. I see his mouth curve up a little as I glance in the rearview mirror from the back seat. He's stiff as a board. I know he's nervous.

"Mrs. McMillan says they've got a big choir," Sharon begins to chatter. "I can't wait till I'm old enough to sing in a choir. I love how they all sing a different line and it all fits together. Miss Satre taught us how to do two parts in fifth and 6th grade . . ." and she keeps the self-conversation going the whole twenty minutes it takes to reach main street. "Wow! look at all the people," she shouts. "No wonder they have to have such a big tent."

We park three blocks away and jostle with the crowd moving toward the tent which is almost as big as the three-ring big top at the circus. Hope there are seats left. Don't know if Tom can stand for two hours. His leg still gives him trouble just standing in one spot.

The smell of the warm evening and the passel of people blends with the thick wood shavings they've spread on the ground. Electric light bulbs hang on black wires down the center aisle. Up front, the choir's singing and people in the audience are humming along. There's a pulpit in the middle of the stage with an extra big light hanging right over it. It's the same atmosphere as Camp Meeting.

Five rows from the back, we find an empty bench with room for us four. Tom, ever the gentleman, let's us girls slide in first. He takes the guard position on the end where he can escape if things get too heavy and he needs to go have a cigarette.

There was little money for luxuries like smoking during the eleven years before he went to work for the railroad. At first he only smoked outside, with friends and neighbors—a social thing, you know. Then it became necessary with his morning coffee. Now it's used to calm his nerves. Isn't my place to fuss. All the men do it. I hate the smell on our clothes and the taste when he kisses me. I don't complain. He's a good husband and father. That's what's important.

The choir stops singing. A tall, bald man in a gray suit steps to the pulpit. "Stand with me as we pray together," he says. The prayer is short. His Amen is immediately followed by a song,

"I am so glad that Jesus loves me, Jesus loves me, Jesus loves,
    I am so glad that Jesus loves me, Jesus loves even me."

There must be hundreds of people here. I bet they can hear us singing all the way down Main Street to Montgomery Wards. It's so uproarious you can't hear yourself sing.

Twenty minutes later, they take an offering to help pay for the campaign's expenses. I'm surprised to see Tom drop a dollar into the bucket as it goes down our row.

"Brothers and Sisters," the song leader announces, "I want to introduce you to the man God chose to bring you Good News tonight, Hyman Appleman." Immediately, a short, stocky man steps up to the pulpit. His booming voice reaches us instantly. After the first few sentences, it becomes easier to translate his words into our Idaho English. His jet-black hair and sparkling brown eyes tell of his Jewish heritage and his accent relays his homeland of Russia.

"Everyone knows the verse John 3:16," he begins. "Let's say it together."

We all chimed in unison, "For God so loved the world that he gave his only begotten Son, that whosoever believeth in him will not perish but have ever lasting life."

"The key word in that verse is 'whosoever'," he continues. "But I want to talk about the next verse. Listen to this: "For God sent not his Son into the world to condemn the world, but that the world through him might be saved. He that believeth on him is not condemned; but he that believeth not is condemned already." He stops waits a few beats then repeats, "'He that believeth on him is not condemned; but he that believeth not is condemned already.' John is telling us the Good News about Jesus. Jesus came because his Father God sent him and together, they flooded the population of the whole world, all the whosoever's, with this great love as Jesus willingly went to the cross to die in my place and your place.

"God loves you. He doesn't judge your life or condemn you because you're a mess. He loves you. He wants you to believe that. It's that simple. You just have to believe. But . . . if you choose not to believe, then you are choosing to be condemned."

I can't believe what I'm hearing. It's like he's talking right to Tom. Tom always says, "God don't want nothing to do with me 'cause I'm a mess." He doesn't think God can possibly love him.

I don't know what else Mr. Appleman says. I'm lost in my own thoughts and prayers.

Suddenly everyone's on their feet singing, "Just as I am without one plea, but that thy blood was shed for me . . ." I feel movement beside me, open my eyes and watch my husband's back moving down the center aisle toward the front. I gasp, squeeze Sharon's hand and follow him.

*   *   *

Tom

It's quiet in the car. Think I shocked my family. Cain't tell 'em how I'm feelin' right now. Sorta like I bin carryin' a fifty-pound sack a flour around and it's done bin unloaded. Don't halfta carry it no more. I'm hangin' tight ta the armrest 'cause I'm feelin' like I'll jest float right ta the roof. Tears nag ta come. Not manly ta cry, my father would say. Don't halfta listen ta his prattle in my brain no more 'cause I've got a new Father. Yes, sir. This Father don't tell me I'm no good. This Father loves me and had his Son killed instead of me. That love's somethin' else. He done it just 'cause. I've stored up a passel of water behind these eyes. I drag out my hanky just in time to catch them tears pourin' down my face.

We sit in our drive. I feel three hands rubbin' my back. I let go the dam. The only sound's my sobbin'. Don't know how long we sit here. I know it's long as it takes to wash away the old man Tom. Appleman prayed fer me ta be a new man. God's adoin' it.

Sobbin' stops. I hear Susie say, "Thank you, Jesus."

Neen adds, "Yes, Jesus. He's yours."

"Now our whole family belongs to you, Jesus." my daughter says.

We climb outa the car and hug long and hard. I get ahold Susie's hand on one side and Sharon's on the other. We walk into our house. I pull out my pack of Camels, walk ta the heatin' stove, open the door and throw 'em in. Yes, sir. I'm a new man.

*   *   *

Didn't Expect This

Sharon

Mom and I prayed as long as I can remember for Dad to ask Jesus into his heart. When it happens, I get excited. No more silent treatment. Dad will be full of joy and peace. He won't lose his temper any more. And most of all, he'll go to church with us on Sundays and we won't have to ride the bus.

Dad works Sundays. So, Mom and I still ride the old yellow bus to The Orchard's Community Church. Sometimes things don't go how you plan.

I'm old enough now for the youth group. Dad doesn't get off work in time for the youth meeting. We don't get there until the evening service starts. I don't get to see my friends any more. Sometimes things don't go how you plan.

Mom's the one I look to for permission. Now, what Dad says is the final answer. Mom says nothing. Sometimes things don't go how you plan.

*   *   *

Susan

I've dreamed of this day; tried to be the bridge between Tom and God. So long. It's been so long. Twenty-five years I practiced patience, waiting for God to move Tom. I thought Sharon would be the influence. Our daughter's half grown before it happens. He's the head of the family. I must let God lead. My husband gets up an hour early every morning and devours his Bible. He reads slow, but he remembers it all. *God, teach Tom. Help me be patient while You lead him.*

Chapter 38

SWIMMING LESSONS

Sharon

School doesn't start for another three weeks. It's hot. Got up to 112° today.

My friend RD calls. "It's so hot, I'm dying. Dad says I should take swimming lessons. Want to come with me?"

Swimming? In the water? My mind flashes back to the ocean where a girl got pulled under by an octopus, to the floods where houses were under water up to their peaks, to the Columbia River rushing over the Celilo Falls where the fisherman would have fallen to his death with one small misstep.

"Uh, I . . . don't know. I've never tried." I answer.

"Me neither," RD says. "Let's give it a try."

"Where?" I was shaking my head thinking of the swift flow of the rivers that run on two sides of Lewiston.

"In the swimming pool at Vollmer Park. My dad'll drive us. Lessons are for two weeks."

Two weeks in the water? I suddenly realize I've been holding my breath like I was already going under. I mustn't let my best friend know I'm afraid.

"All right," I finally respond. "Let me ask Mom."

"Tell her you have to have a suit and a swim cap," RD adds.

"OK, just a minute." I lay down the phone and find Mom in the kitchen. "Mom, RD wants me to go to the pool with her to take swim lessons. I need a suit and a swim cap. Her dad will take us." I'm shaking my head, but Mom doesn't look up from the bread she's kneading.

"I think that's a good idea. With all the water we have around here, it's important you learn to swim. I swam in the pond on the farm a little when I was a kid. Tell her yes," she answers and continues making her bread. I'm still shaking my head when I get back to the phone.

"Mom says yes," I tell her.

"Great. Lessons start Monday. We'll pick you up at nine o'clock." The click of the receiver sets me shivering. What did I just get myself into?

*   *   *

Monday morning, I sit on the front step beside Lassie and tell her how scared I am. I have on my swim suit under my dress and my cap and towel are in my hand. Dad would have a fit if he saw how much skin my suit shows. Pastor Crouse and RD pull up right on time. I give Lassie one long hug hoping it won't be the last.

The pool's huge. I drop my clothes along the fence, put my towel on top, stretch the rubber cap over my head and stand with the other kids along the end of the pool. Our instructor is Dale. He looks like he's still in high school. I'm amazed our teacher's so young. He blows his whistle.

"All right. You're all beginners here. So, we'll start in the shallow end. Be careful when you walk down the steps. They're slippery." I follow the crowd of to-be swimmers into the water, hoping I can fake liking the wet stuff that's now up to my knees. I slowly move to the right and grab onto the edge.

"You, there in the white cap, you're too tall for that depth. You need to move down here in front of me." I slosh through the cool wetness until I can find a space next to the wall. When I turn around, the instructor is standing in front of me.

Oh no, he'll be able to watch me like a hawk. I can't do this. I just can't do this.

I'm shaking like it's dead of winter. It's already 95 degrees on the big thermometer at the end of the pool. I glance at RD two people down from me. She smiles and looks back at the instructor.

"You're lighter in the water," he's saying. "If you let yourself relax, you'll feel your body rising to the top of the water. Turn around, hold on to the edge, relax and let your feet drift up of the bottom of the pool."

What? No way am I going to let my feet get off the bottom of the pool. I become a stick, ridged and unbendable.

"Relax, relax," he says as he goes under the water and moves my legs off the floor. I scream and scramble up and over the edge of the pool. Don't ask me how. Suddenly, I'm on the warm concrete. Still shivering.

"I'm sorry, I'm sorry . . ." he apologizes. "Sit and watch for a while. You'll see how easy it is."

I want to yell, WATER DESTROYS, WATER PULLS YOU UNDER, WATER KILLS. I sit in silence and watch. Yes, it's easy for them. They look like they're enjoying it, but they haven't seen what I've seen. They don't know.

I get brave enough to dangle my feet in the water. The instructor is already moving on to step two: letting go of the edge. Dale looks at me, smiles and motions for me to get in the water. I slide down in, grab hold of the edge and let my feet drift up. I have enough stubborn Chase blood in me to decide this is dumb behavior and I can do it. Hm. It does feel good. I've never actually been in water deeper than twelve inches in our bath tub. Maybe, maybe I'll fill the tub and get the feel of it there. I get brave enough to let go for a second. My body starts to turn. I panic and grab hold.

*   *   *

The second day goes better. We stand, lay back and float. Well, at least I try. I sink to the bottom every time.

"Lift your hips. Take a deep breath. Keep your body still," Dale yells at me. Over and over, I attempt to do what he says. I think I'm a natural bottom feeder. Or maybe I have a sinker on my line with no bobber. It just doesn't work.

Day after day, Dale patiently tries to help me. With ten other kids, he can't spend much time on just me. By the end of the first week, RD is doing a back stroke and I'm still attempting to float. This is not going well.

At the end of the second week, I do the back stroke, float, and find my way to the top every time I sink to the bottom. Well, I guess that's some progress. I decide I'm never going to be good at this. I don't plan to come back. I make a decision: Stay away from water.

Chapter 39

1952, FALL 7TH GRADE

No, I didn't get anything Jantzen. Not enough money. I shop with Mom. That means three suitable dresses for school and the hot weather we're having. I'll wait until I sell my sheep this fall to get my dream clothes. I haven't grown this year so don't need a new coat. My sheep money will buy that Jantzen sweater and skirt that will help me fit in with the town kids. It's too hot to wear wool now anyway.

Getting up an hour earlier is for the birds ... not for me. Ha, ha. Get it. I love to sleep. To catch the bus to the Junior High, I have to rise and shine. This is the first time Mom and Dad haven't gone with me on the first day of school. The bus rattles down Grelle and Thain and sucks in about forty kids. Most of them I know.

RD saves a place for me. We compare class cards we got in the mail.

"Look at that," I cry. "We only have math and social studies together. I bet they separated us on purpose. It's not fair."

"It's okay." RD smiles. "You'll know somebody in class. I've moved several times and gone to different schools. I always find a friend. I found you, didn't I?"

I shrug my shoulders. "I guess so." We file off the bus and say goodbye until math time.

They sent a map with our cards. Classes are in two different buildings. One of them is the Old Webster School where I went to fourth grade. At least I know where to find the bathrooms there. My first hour class is a half-underground room at the front of the Junior High Building. I peek in.

My teacher's old, gray haired, and square built. She wears a grumpy face, looks at me and waves me in. I find a seat in front of Sandy. At least I know one person here. She's not a friend. She's the one I pulled the piano stool out from under when she wouldn't let me have a turn. I still feel guilty. I know she hates me, even though it's been five years.

The screeching bell nearly sends me under my desk. What a horrible sound. I cover my ears and close my eyes. How often does that happen?

"All right, children," Mrs. Peterson begins (Children? I'm not a child anymore.). "I'm Mrs. Peterson, your Home Room teacher. I will also be your Home Ec teacher. During home room we get the day started with flag salute, Bible reading, and announcements. Then we do the subject of English. All stand."

After the flag salute I start to sing "Oh, say can you see . . ." Everyone giggles. I don't see what's so funny. We always sing after the pledge. Obviously not here. I turn red and sit.

"We don't sing in this class," Mrs. Peterson says. I see a hint of a smile. She reads from the Psalms. "Now let me tell you how this works." She shoves her pink rimmed glasses up on top of her head. "We'll study English for this hour. When the bell rings you take your book and go to your next class. You don't all go to the same class, so you have to figure out where you belong. Check your card. It has the time and room number on it. You only have five minutes to get to your next class. Do you understand?"

We all nod.

"Very well," she nods back. Here's your English book. Bert and James, would you come help pass these out? I'm going to call your name. You give me the number inside the front."

The book is thick and heavy. I have five classes with books. If every class book is this big, how will I be able to carry all of them?

"This is your assignment for today: write something about yourself you'd like me to know. There's only a half hour of class left."

How can I possibly write it all in a half hour? I write fast and furious. I'm not done when the horrible bell screeches. We pile our papers on her desk and go on the hunt for the next class. Mine's math, second floor, room 201. Mrs. Wishard.

This building seems as old as Old Webster. The stairs creak and the banisters are worn smooth by years of hands. Ah, there it is, right at the top of the stairs. There's RD. Good. We sit one behind the other.

"Who's your Home Room?" I whisper. "Do you know anyone in it?"

"Mr. Cravens," she whispers back. "Two people." The bell screeches.

"I'm Mrs. Wishard," this blond, curly-haired teacher begins. "You will not dilly dally in the hall. If you come in after the bell, you'll go to the office to get a tardy slip. We will start promptly. You two girls pass out the Math Books." She points at RD and me and to the stack of books. It's not quite as big as the English but it's heavy. Again, we give the number in the book when she calls our name.

"Now class, get a piece of paper from your notebook. This is how you will prepare every paper in this class. Name in the upper right-hand corner, under it Class 2, under it the date, then under it Test number 1. Yes, I want to know what skills you have in math. Today you'll be taking a test." She smiles at our gasps.

A test? The first day of school?

"You have a half hour to finish. If you finish early there'll be no talking. Check your work.

"In the back of your book are the tests you'll be taking each week. Turn to page one-thirty-five in your text. You will write the number, the problem and then work the problem. Any questions? I should think not. Ready? Start."

Math's not my best subject. There's forty-five problems. The first row is addition, second is subtraction. Next, multiplication, then a row of division. Last . . . oh, no, the dreaded story problems. I hate story problems. I work as fast as I can. I know I'll be slow on the story problems. Time's up before I finish.

I'm not sure how to handle this rush, rush, rush. I've always finished first in my class. Now I can't get anything finished. I'm a failure and we've only had two hours of school. Physical Education, Social Studies, US history, Home Economics and Band yet to go. Whew!

*   *   *

Boy. Physical education, they call it PE, is a whole new thing. We have uniforms. Mom and I went to Penny's store where they sell "regulation" blue shorts and white, snap down the front, sleeveless shirts. Shorts? I've never been allowed to wear shorts. My dad would have a tizzy if he saw me in those. It was bad enough when I had to have a swim suit for lessons. He allowed it because I'd be under water.

He says, "Nice girls don't wear clothes showin' their legs up high and my daughter's a nice girl." Thank goodness he won't be at school. We're not allowed to participate in PE without shorts. We also buy white canvas tennis shoes to be worn only when we're in the gym. These clothes cost half of what my Jantzen skirt and sweater will. Seems like a waste of money to me.

I've been carrying my uniform and gym shoes in a sack. Mrs. Long comes in the dressing room and assigns us a locker to put them in.

"You'll have ten minutes to change into your uniform before going to the gym," she tells us. "You'll put your clothes in your locker during class. When we're finished, put your gym shoes on the bottom of your locker and fold your uniform and put it on the top shelf. On the last day of the week, take your uniform home for your mom to wash and iron it. Bring it back the day of first class. At the end of every class, you must take a shower before getting dressed. Towels are stacked over there by the door. Put them in the bag by the outside door when you're finished. These rules are important and will be part of your grade for the class."

Because of all the instructions for the first day, we do a practice run of what the class time looks like. There's no privacy. This is so embarrassing. I'm an only child. I've never seen anyone in their underwear and no one's seen me in mine. That makes me a speedy dresser.

The absolute worst is after class. We have to take a shower in a big room with sprayers around it. Stripped bare-naked! This is the ultimate mortification. I get in, out, and dressed in record time. Can't say I get very wet. Water again holds terror for me. Why we have to do this is never explained. All my life I've taken a bath on Saturday night—in private. I'm determined to be the fastest dresser ever. How humiliating! Thank goodness, PE's only Mondays and Wednesdays.

Tuesdays and Thursdays are Home Ec. I'll love that class. We'll learn to sew—on an electric machine. Mom has a treadle. I tried to sew pot holders for Christmas presents on it. It takes good coordination between hands, and feet. Can't go very fast.

Fridays, I go back to Home Room for Citizenship Class. Not sure what that's all about. Mrs. Peterson says it's very important.

It's time to eat. I'm starved. It's been five hours since breakfast. They call it lunch break. I've been tempted to sneak something out of my lunch pail, but there's not been time. I'm sure going to get muscles carrying around all these books, my clarinet, clothes, and lunch. We're supposed to eat across the street in the high school cafeteria. It's big enough to hold all of us. It's so noisy RD and I can hardly hear each other.

"Let's go outside and have a picnic," I shout to RD. She nods. We sit on the grass. "Ah, much better. So tell me about your classes. Have you had PE yet?"

Lunch time seems shorter than class times. Again, it's rush rush, rush, eat fast and back to the next class—US History. Mr. Hays is tall, skinny and has a crooked smile that he throws at us.

"What you'll get in here is a mixture of History and Geography. They go hand in hand. You have to know the place before you can know what happened there." He talks like he loves this subject. He adds another book to my stack.

Social Studies is taught by my cousin's husband, Mr. Cravens. I don't know him very well. At least he knows who I am. We get another big book. I'm thinking it's going to be a subject I like. I'm a social person. I'm glad RD's in this class. We can study together. I recognize many kids in this class. Most are in Band.

Before class is over, Mr. Cravens says, "Bring everything and come with me." We follow him into the hall. He points to a row of lockers along the wall under the stairs. I've been so busy trying to find classes I hadn't noticed them.

"You'll be assigned a locker with another person," he instructs. "You may put your books in there so you don't have to carry them around all day. You can take them home to do your assignments.

They're your responsibility. If you lose them, you'll have to pay for them. There's a place to hang your coats too. You'll decide with your locker mate, who takes the top and who gets the bottom."

Oh, I hope I get RD as my locker mate. We get along so good.

"As I read off the numbers and names go stand by your locker." He begins, reading only last names: "Number two-twenty-one, Chase, Dyer …" Oh no that's me and … and … the girl who hates me. This can't be right. I dutifully walk over and stand by Sandy.

"Top or bottom," I ask. She points up. I put my books in the bottom and stand with the rest of the class.

God has a sense of humor. Still holding my clarinet case, I glance down and see Sandy's holding a clarinet case too. Yes, God has a sense of humor and I think he's trying to tell me something.

I trudge across the gravel parking lot and up the squeaky stairs to the third-floor band room at Old Webster School. I'll face competition for seating in the clarinet section. I must do my best so I don't have to sit by her.

I sit by the window in the very quiet bus. Exhaustion overcomes me. I lean my head on the window thinking, *I have so much to tell Mama on the blue stool today.*

Chapter 40

THIS IS HARD

Sharon

I'm not handling this Junior High stuff very well. It's rush, rush, rush; switch—body and brain. No recesses, little time to eat, no time to relax. And the noise—awk! The bell, the scooch of chairs, the creaky old buildings, the stomping feet up and down stairs, talking, yelling. It's driving me crazy. And people? These people around me, all the time? They're rude, obnoxious and don't care about anything except themselves. Disgusting!

RD and I sit on the low cement wall and wait for our bus to arrive.

"You know what?" I explode a big breath. "If I ever become a teacher, I never, never want to teach this age. I don't even like myself."

She laughs, "Oh, you'll get used to it. My brother at thirteen was terrible. He was so mean. Now, he's a pretty nice guy." Her brother's a senior in high school. He's almost a grown up.

"I know," I admit. "We'll change. If I taught this age, I'd be stuck with Junior-Hitis all day. I can't stand me; how would I stand them." We both laugh. We like to make up new words. I sober up quick, "How are we ever going to get through this?"

"Together," she sighs.

*   *   *

I had a ton of rock unloaded on me today. It's called my dad's heavy foot. He slammed it down on my feet.

"NO, NO, NEVER, NEVER WILL MY DAUGHTER DANCE! he shouts when I ask my parents to sign the permission slip. They're going to start teaching dance in PE. We must have our parent's okay.

"Dancin's a devil's thing and you ain't gonna do it. End of discussion." He's still shouting.

"Dad . . ." I begin.

"I don't wanna hear it." He walks out the door.

"Mom . . ." I look at her with pleading eyes.

"We have to follow what your father says. I'm sorry." Mom looks so sad I don't have the heart to beg any more. Guess that settles it.

I take my slip to the PE teacher. There's a big NO written on it in ink. How embarrassing. I sit on a bench and watch everyone having a great time. I love the music. It's called, "In the Mood." My body's in the mood. It wants to move. My mind is confused and angry. *I don't understand this, Jesus. I bet you danced at that wedding where you changed the water to wine. I thought life was going to be easier when Dad became your child.*

*   *   *

Mom's Uncle Willie starts meetings at the Sommerville Home about a mile from our place. Up until last year, it was called the County Old Folk's Home or the Poor House. It's where old people go who don't have anyone to take care of them.

"We're goin' out there and help Willie" Dad says. "Sharon, ya need ta work on sum hymns on that pianer sos ya can play for the singin'."

It's not a question. It's a command. I feel a knot in my stomach. Every day, I sit at the piano, find all the hymns in the key of C, and practice, practice, practice. I'm so nervous.

Thursday, after supper, we drive to a brick building in the middle of the wheat field. "Glad to have you come along," Uncle Willie pats me on the shoulder. "Having a young, pretty piano player will brighten their day."

"I hope it's okay I can only play a few songs," I apologize. "I'm new at this."

"Don't matter," he grins. "Most of these people don't remember week to week even who I am. They live in the now."

We enter a big room with chairs around the edge. Every chair's full. Uncle Willie introduces Dad and me. They clap and cheer. I sit at the piano. My hands shake. We start with "I Am a Child of God." The people sing, not so much together, but from their heart. It's loud. I don't think they hear all the wrong notes I hit. I relax and concentrate on the music. It's going to be okay. I glance at Dad. He's beaming.

*   *   *

Milan rides bus No. 13, too. It's funny how he's been in the desk behind me in every class since third grade. He grabs a seat in back of RD and me on the bus. He's smarter than me in math. I can't compete there. In other subjects we push each other. He's in my Sunday School classes too. His dad has a tractor. My dad hires him to plow our garden every year and cut and rake our alfalfa. Our families are friends.

Now Milan's irritating. I want to talk to RD. Milan keeps playing with my curls or leaning up and interrupting our conversation. I try to ignore and yet be polite. Mama's always told me to be polite.

"Have you heard of Youth for Christ?" RD asks. "My brother's going to lead part of the program Saturday night."

"Heard about it; never been." I admit. "What do they do?"

"It's all run by youth." She gets animated. "No adults. The youth plan, lead music, pray, and even speak. Sometimes they have special guest speakers like Tex Yearout. The music's all choruses. No hymns. They have youth sing specials like solos, trios and quartets. There's even a youth choir in summer when there's time to practice. This Saturday's at the Assembly of God on 21st Street. I'd ask you to come with us, but our car's full. Ask your folks to take you?"

RD's excitement is catching. "I'll ask."

"Me too." I hear Milan's voice behind us as he leans against the back of our seat. "See if your dad'll take me too."

*   *   *

"Now that's sumthin' I'd be happy to take ya to," Dad responds when I ask.

"Uh, would you mind picking up Milan?" I add. I hope he says he can't.

"We can do that." Dad says.

That's the beginning of our Saturday night ritual. Our car becomes three across in the front and stacked two-deep in the back seat as we stop along the way and pick up kids. Not much breathing room with nine good sized bodies. How Dad concentrates on driving, I don't know. We tell jokes, laugh and sing. We have to leave an hour early sometimes because YFC is never at the same church. Picking up kids takes time.

Patty and Nancy are at Youth for Christ too. They're both in some of my classes. They've been good friends a long time like RD and me. We sit together. They become a good addition to our lunch time chats.

I meet this good-looking blond guy in my Social Studies class. His name's Ralph. He's . . . different. He wears his hair slicked back, jeans, a white t-shirt and doesn't have a coat. Says he never gets cold. He's very nice to me. I love his smile.

One day, I ask. "Would you like to go to Youth for Christ with us on Saturday night? Milan, Jake and Margaret always go with us. Dad drives. We could pick you up."

"Sure," he answers. "Long as it's not church."

Hmmm. I'm thinking. Really, it's not what you'd call church.

We add Ralph to our crowd. He and Milan become good friends. Our YFC car gang plus RD's car gang along with Patty and Nancy, begin to hang out together at school. It's March. I finally feel like I have a place I belong. I hardly ever see my Orchard's School friends—never Cody. I still have his ID bracelet.

*   *   *

It's May. I'm used to the noises, the rush, the pace of school. I'll never be used to attitudes.

RD and I sit on the wall, as usual, waiting for the bus. Behind us, there's an outbreak of yelling, name calling, and what sounds like fists hitting bodies. We jump up. I'm shocked to see Milan and Ralph having a knock-down, drag-out fight, right here in front of the building. Milan's nose pours red and Ralph's split lip is double in size. What on earth?

"Hey, you two. Stop it. Stop! Stop!" I'm screaming.

A crowd gathers. I hear a man's voice coming from the front door. "Boys! Both of you. Up to the office." They stop. Look at each other, follow the voice into the building, turn, point at me and then themselves. What?

I don't see either guy, except at a distance, the rest of the year. They avoid me and each other. Rumors say the fight was over me. I have no idea. They must have decided I wasn't worth the trouble they got into.

*   *   *

I hesitate to even write this. I've always been a good girl, done the right thing. Never even walk on someone's lawn.

Mom says, "They worked hard to make it beautiful. You mustn't walk on it."

I don't remember a rebellious thought before. Well . . . except the marble tournament in fourth grade, and bumping Judy off the tetter totter . . . oh and pulling the stool out from under Sandy. This is different. Maybe it's spring fever. Maybe it's my age; secretly wanting to become one of them.

While waiting for the bus today, I say to RD, "I wonder what it feels like to skip school."

"I've wondered that too." She looks at me. "Do you think it would be fun or would you feel guilty?"

"I guess we'll never know . . . unless we . . ." We look at each other and smile.

"Tomorrow?" she asks.

I nod. "Bring money."

I admit I don't sleep well. There's excitement, anticipation, planning. I get up early, dress in my favorite sleeveless dress with scarecrows all around the bottom, and put on good walking shoes. Fifth hour. It will happen fifth hour.

Concentration is hard. Time drags, It's Thursday. If we don't get caught, maybe they'll forget we weren't there for two hours.

Finally, fifth hour, my Home Ec time. We're sewing aprons. I become very industrious. Suddenly I clamp my hand over my mouth, make my eyes go big and rush over to Mrs. Peterson.

"Mrs. Peterson." I muffle. "I think I swallowed a pin. It was in my mouth while I was pinning the ruffle. I coughed and felt something sharp and now it's gone. I need to go." I run out of the room before she can say anything and meet RD in the hallway. We rush out the door, across the parking lot and walk leisurely down the hill to our destination—Albertson's grocery store. We giggle, laugh and talk about how easy it was. RD simply told her teacher she was going to throw up. No teacher wants to clean that up.

There's a long, food counter. I already know what I want. RD orders a banana split. I get a hot fudge sundae. We take our time eating and talking; not about what we've done. We pretend we're two adults out for a treat.

Time's up. We have a bus to catch. Trudging back up the steep hill, we talk about how easy it is to do the wrong thing.

"Yup. It was pretty easy," I say. "Exciting even, but I don't want to do it again."

"Agree," RD grins. "I won't make it a habit." We both know the consequences at home if our parents find out.

Our bus pulls up. We sit, silent in our own thoughts. I wonder what will happen tomorrow. Will I ever tell anyone what I did?

No one says a word the next day. It's been a permanent secret. Until I just told you.

Chapter 41

A Tragic Summer

Sharon

Dad gets a shift change and has Sundays and Mondays off. That means he'll go to church with us on Sunday morning too. This is great! Now I'll get to go to the Youth Group with my friends Sunday nights.

"I've been thinkin'," Dad says as we're getting ready for church. I freeze. When he says, 'I've been thinking' it means there's going to be a change.

"I've been thinkin' we oughta try out the Church of God in Clarkston," he finishes.

"Clarkston? That's in a whole different state. I don't even know anyone there. It'll take hours to get there. Are you sure? I want to go to the Youth Group at Orchards." I throw out my immediate pleas.

It's like he doesn't even hear my protests. "Yep, the church where Mama and us kids went in Stites. Your mama went when the traveling minister came. My sister's church. Susie's aunts too. It's where we belong."

I look at Mom. She's smiling. I go in my room, shut the door and burst into tears. They don't understand. I need to be with my friends. I'll be an outcast if I go to church in Clarkston. They won't like me at that church because I go to Lewiston school. At school, they won't like me 'cause I'm a traitor going to church in our rival, Clarkston. When my tears quit coming, it dawns on me: I do have friends in Clarkston.

I've met some at Youth for Christ. I wash my face, take a big breath, go out and say, "Okay, I'm ready."

I'm right. It takes forty-five minutes to get there. We have to drive downtown, across the only bridge to Clarkston, then to ninth and diagonal. We're late.

Dad's right too. We know people there. Family, family, family. I bet half the people there are related to us.

The pastor's name is E. Dewey Johnson. Hm. Wonder what the E stands for? He's about as tall as Dad but only half as wide. His black-rimmed glasses match his hair and mustache. He talks very fast. People lean to listen, 'cause ears have a hard time listening fast. His beautiful, blond wife, Ailene, plays the organ. I think she must come from the south 'cause her talk sounds the same way as my grandma's Alabama neighbors. Mom says they have a boy named Neil. They adopted him when he was a baby.

Another blond lady named Adeline plays the piano. Man, can she play! I'm fascinated by what she does on those keys. The singing's amazing. People sing at the top of their lungs like they did at Camp Meeting. I had no idea people sing that way in common everyday church.

The amazing thing is how people talk during the sermon. There's constant "Amen. Preach it brother. Yes, it is. Tell the truth. You're right. Hallelujah." It's shocking. I'd never interrupt a preacher. The more they do it, the faster he talks. I guess he's used to it. It's like their words wind him up.

The church is full. Dad says there's at least three hundred people there. Everyone wants to talk afterward. The Curtis' family invites us to dinner. Mom knows them from growing up in the Reuben's area.

Okay, this might not be a bad move.

*　　*　　*

Mom sits on the edge of my bed like she does every night to tell me good night. She brushes her hand across my hair. Tears fill her dark, brown eyes.

"What's wrong, Mama?" I reach up and hug her. I seldom see her cry. She's a strong woman. I want to be like her.

"It's about Patty," she chokes out. "She's run away, got married to a sailor, and gone to San Diego."

"What? Mama . . . no . . . Patty wouldn't do that. She just finished tenth grade. She's got to go to school. Why would she do such a thing?" My heart's in my throat. A sailor? Is she going to live on a boat? I reel with the thought of what's going to happen to my only cousin in Mom's family.

I've been busy adjusting to Junior High. I've not seen or talked to her except at Christmas when we had dinner at their house. Everything seemed fine. She'd painted her bedroom walls black and the trim, bed frame and dresser turquoise. Aunt Edna made a bedspread and curtains out of turquoise and silver satin. It's the neatest thing I've ever seen. Why would she leave all that?

"I don't know, honey." Mom answers after a long silence. "Edna couldn't explain. Grandma and Grandpa are heart-broken. We need to pray for everyone."

Neither of us can pray out loud. I feel Mom leave and hear a sob as she closes my door. I cry myself to sleep. Patty's the closest thing I've ever had to a sister.

*   *   *

Dad drops us off at Grandma and Grandpa's on his way to work at 6:00 a.m. The berries have to be picked before it gets too hot. Patty's eloped and Aunt Edna's cooking the breakfast lunch shift at Jack's Place. There's only four of us picking. We work fast to finish the patch before the weekend. Grocery stores aren't open on Sunday.

Sunday afternoon, Grandma calls. "Susie, some bad news about your cousin, Genevieve Simmons. She went swimming in the horse pond on their ranch. Now she's in the hospital with polio. They've had to put her in an iron lung to help her breathe. She's real bad. They don't think she'll make it."

I don't know Genevieve. I met her once at a Kole/Denney reunion in Reubens. I think she graduated a few years ago. I know she's younger than Mom.

Polio's all around us. They're saying it's something in the water. There you go again, water. Don't go in the water. Water is dangerous.

Again, Grandma and Grandpa have a big hurt. It's a sad June.

*   *   *

Fourth of July celebration is at our house every year. Both sides of my family fill our shady front yard for a big picnic. After dark, Dad sets off Roman candles and fountains in the alfalfa field; we all have sparklers and sing "God Bless America."

Dad and I set up sawhorses with planks on top for a food table and bring out chairs from the house. I'm taking out the last chair. The phone rings. Mom answers.

"Tom! It's Neen," she shouts through the screen door. "She's very upset."

"Hello," I watch Dad's face pale as he listens to his sister, "No, no, no. Oh, no. Oh, Sis. Where are you? We'll be right there."

"What's happened?" Mom asks. "I couldn't understand a word through her sobs."

"Otis had a heart attack. She drove him to the hospital but it was too late. He's gone."

My tiny uncle is twenty years older than Aunt Neen. I'm actually taller than him. At seventy-two, he still raises fruits and vegetables he sells in town. I work with him when we stop to visit. He talks to me like I'm an adult. Just the two of us—picking, trimming berries and trees, pulling weeds. Gone. No, he can't just leave without saying goodbye.

Mom and Dad rush to the hospital to be with Aunt Neen. I sit and cry.

*   *   *

It's August. We've been going to the Church of God for Sunday School and church in the morning and Youth Group and church at night. I discover LeRoy Nick, my Junior High principal, is the Sunday School superintendent. It's nice to know he's a Christian. Alvin and Jacquie Hanks lead the youth group. They're a young couple who don't have kids yet. Most of the youth are much older than me, but they make me feel at home.

Alvin says, "Hey Sharon, I hear you play the piano."

I laugh, "As long as it's in the key of C."

They pick songs out of the hymnal in the key of C and I play along. I've not practiced much this last year with all the Junior-Hitis going on. I have to get busy and work on other chords.

Before school starts, the youth and Sunday School classes have a party at Beach View Park.

"I don't want to go," I tell Mom. "I don't like being close to water." She doesn't push me. I'm relieved.

At four o'clock, we get a phone call from Mom's Aunt Ada. "Pray for the Johnsons. Their son, Neil, drowned swimming in the Snake River during the party this afternoon."

None of us can speak. What? He's only ten years old. Wanted so much he was adopted. You're supposed to be old when you die. Now there's two kids I know died in the water. This summer's been the saddest time of my whole life. Don't trust the water.

*   *   *

Susan

It's a grim summer. A summer full of bereavement. It tests my bridge, my faith, my understanding. It seems no matter how hard I try to help, to listen, to work, to let God do what he wants to do, there's nothing but hurting.

Tough times in my life involved only Tom and me. No one to talk to, just God and me.

Now hard things are hitting people we love. I don't know how to face them. I don't know what to say. It's like a whirlpool sucking me under. It blocks out life like the dark closet blocked out reality when I was hiding from Tom's menacing father.

I'm not good at expressing feelings. Maybe it's a problem of trust. People won't take me seriously. They'll laugh, mock me like my mother did, or pat my back and say it's going to be all right. Maybe it's pride. I'll be seen as weak. Not able to handle life. Maybe there aren't any words I know to tell other people how I feel. I'm speechless.

I've noticed Sharon responds the same way. When she's upset, she shuts herself in her room. I hear her sobs. Should I go and talk? Should I let her cry it out? What can I say that will do any good? We're in an earthquake. How do I keep my bridge steady?

Chapter 42

PUSHING ON

Sharon in band uniform

Sharon

Tragedy. Such a disastrous summer. Our quiet house hears little conversation. No laughter. Things pile on one another. My safe, sheltered life shatters. Unexpected events and bad choices break people and silence the world. Life'll never be the same. I walk on tip toes. I must be good, follow the rules, do the right thing. "Keeping safe in Jesus," Mom calls it.

It's a relief to go back to school where no one knows my gloomy soul. It's easier to put a smile on my face and laugh at corny jokes. Life in motion. Life moving on. I can escape here because no one knows. No one recognizes the storm brewing inside. A storm that leaves my pillow soaked every night with released emotions. Will the sun ever shine again?

I throw myself into classes. Same subjects, harder challenges.

I watch people come and go.

Patty comes back. Her marriage annulled. She's distant. Doesn't want to talk. Embarrassed? Frightened? Angry? I don't know. I only know our relationship changed.

Marvin, Jensen's son, quit school and joins the Navy.

Phyllis Adams and her mom move downtown close to the high school.

The Johnsons leave and go to Arizona. Ailene's deep in grief and can't stand this place. Mom calls it an emotional breakdown. She needs to get away from reminders of Neil.

Retired preachers give sermons. Other things in the large congregation are held together by regular people.

Uncle Johnny and Aunt Alice move their trailer in back of Grandma and Grandpa's house. They say to help out. Grandma turns 82 in November and Grandpa is 75. Funny how my aunt and uncle never offered help before. Mom says it's because Johnny lost his job and they need a place to live. Grandpa sells the east side of their ten acres to the Huntleys, who build a house right by the driveway. Close neighbors now.

Rosenkranzs sell their big house across Grelle to the Reagans. Boy, do they need it. They have nine boys and a baby girl. They fill every room.

All this coming and going whirls around me but doesn't touch me. I'm numb. I protect myself. Don't let anything or anyone in.

* * *

The Hair Has to Go

Sharon

"Mom, these ringlets have got to go. They make me look like a little girl. I want a short haircut like everyone else." I'm sitting on the blue stool watching her put a roast in the oven.

"Hmm. I suppose we could get Maude to do that. You know once you cut it, you'll need a perm?" I nod. Mom had ringlets like mine until she was five. Her mother whacked them off with farm shears. Her hair went straight. For years, Mom used a curling iron, heated on the wood stove, to wave it. Now she gets a permanent about every three months.

I've gone with Mom when she gets a cut and perm. Maude cuts her hair to just the right length, puts horrid smelling stuff on each section, wraps a tissue paper around it, then rolls it on tiny clips. She dabs each one with the smelly again. Mom sits by the big machine that looks like Medusa's hair. Maude clamps one of the snake's mouths on each curl and let's sizzle 'til the bell goes off. She unclamps, unrolls, shampoos; re-rolls and sticks her under the hair dryer. The whole process takes two stinky hours. I know what I'm in for.

"I'll call and see when we can get an appointment." Mom smiles, "How short do you want it?"

"Like yours," I quickly answer. I'm excited. I'm going to look old enough to be in eighth grade. I've been five foot six inches since sixth grade. I'm a giant with a little girl head.

Dad takes me to Maude's Beauty shop on Friday. My friends at church will be the first to see my grown-up hair.

"I'm gonna visit Neen," Dad says as I get out of the car. "Back in a couple hours."

I wave and head in. Maude's working on a lady with white hair. I sit and read a magazine about keeping a better house. They have to tell people how to do that? Our house is spic and span clean all the time. Mom sweeps, mops, waxes, scrubs sinks, the bathtub; washes windows, clothes and dishes. I dry dishes, dust, fold clothes.

Last week, we got a roll-out rug in the living room and a vacuum cleaner. How much better can you keep your house? I notice the houses in this magazine don't look like ours. They're big, have fancy furniture, and carpet everywhere. Even the ceiling lights are like some fancy ball room. Maybe better doesn't mean cleaner?

"Sharon." Maude brings me out of my Better Housekeeping thoughts. "So, we're going to cut off your curls? We'll save one for you. Are you going to miss them?"

"Nope, I'm ready for grown up hair. I want short, tight curls like Mom's so I need a perm too."

"You have natural curls. Are you sure you want a perm? I have to warn you. It'll be very tight."

"That's what I want." I give her a definite nod.

Two hours later, Dad picks up a different looking girl holding a box with her first cut curl in it.

"Goodness gracious, must be in the wrong place. I'm 'spose to pick up Sharon. Ya' seen her?" he asks Maude.

"Dad ..." Everyone laughs.

My dark, curled-tight hair looks painted on my head. It'll take some getting used to.

I walk in our door and Mom's crying. "What's wrong? Are you okay?" Mom never cries— well, not at least in front of me.

"Oh, honey, I'm being silly. I'm sad my little girl's growing up."

"Yaa ... aa ... ah" I respond slowly. "Isn't that what I'm 'spose to do?"

"Of course, it is." she gives me a long Mama hug. It will be the last of my little girl hugs.

I don't comb my new curls until Sunday morning. I want them perfect. Sleeping messes them up, even though I put on one of Mom's hair nets. Comb? No way it'll go through. I take a brush to them. Hair springs up all over my head—frizz. My head's a ball of frightened cat fur sticking out every direction. It's awful. I try water. It bounces back to a fuzz ball. What am I going to do with this mop? Mom can't tame it either. I wear a hat to church even if it isn't Easter.

Everyone keeps saying, "Take off the hat. I want to see. It can't be that bad." I refuse. Maybe a week at home will help it settle down. I sulk in my room.

*　　*　　*

"I'm not going to school." I grump at my mom when she comes to see why I'm not up the first day of school. My alarm clock is the beating of the pancake batter in the kitchen on the other side of the wall. "I'm not getting up."

"Your choice," Mom responds. "I think you'll be sorry you miss the first day of school."

How can I face the teasing; the snide remarks. They already think I'm an oddball. I've proven it with this dumb idea. Why did I ever think this would make life better?

There's a rule in my house: If I'm too sick to go to school, I'm too sick to get out of bed. I resign myself to bed all day. I try to figure out a solution.

"Mom, can I have some paper and a pencil?" At least I can write. I think better when I write. I make a list of things my hair looks like:

a frightened cat
a dandelion gone to seed
a porcupine
a cotton ball
a cottonwood tree
a longhaired, wet dog
an exploded ping pong ball

My list grows through the day.

What am I going to do? I'm so mad at myself. I flop on my side and doze off. A dream creeps into my irritated mind. I'm with John Newman, a missionary who comes to the Orchard's Community Church every other year. He lives in Africa where he tells people how much God loves them. He shows pictures on a screen of God's people in that country. They're smiling, waving, dancing. They love God like I do and... and... and they have hair that looks like mine. Look how beautiful they are. God loves them with their fuzzy hair.

"Yes," I say to myself. "God loves me with fuzzy hair too." I wake up smiling. No matter what people say, I know God loves me, puff ball and all.

Chapter 43

INJURIES OF THE YEAR

Sports, music and my youth group tie me to a purpose. I learn to play tennis and whiffle-ball, but soccer becomes my release. I love the aggression, the fast pace. It's a way to "let off steam," as Dad would say.

Our last game's in Pullman today. It's for the championship.

I hear Mom and Dad cheering our team on. "You've got it. Keep going. You can do this."

We're ahead by two points. Times almost up. The ball's loose in the middle of the field. I scramble after it. So does a Pullman player. Intent, bent low and unaware of the other, we collide head-on and fall flat. Ow!

I watch my teammate shuffle the ball down to the field and slam it in for a goal. The buzzer rings. We scream. "We win!"

Running off the field, I trip, almost fall, then realize I can only see with one eye. The other's a big swollen blob.

The coach finds ice. "Here." She wraps it in a shirt and hands it to me. "Hold this on it. It'll help the swelling." Well, I think it's a bit late for that.

After the game, Dad drives to the church youth rally in Moscow only fifteen minutes away. We have these once a quarter at one of the churches in Moscow, Orofino, Lapwai or Clarkston. We call it Clearwater District Youth. Host church's juniors and seniors do the planning. Each church provides special music. I'm singing today.

"Are you sure you want to go?" Mom questions. "That's a bad bruise. We can go on home."

"It doesn't hurt. I'm fine." I won't admit if it does hurt. After all, I want to be strong like Mom. She never complains.

There's lots of questions and teasing at the rally. I've never had so much attention.

*   *   *

The first Monday of every month there's another sport I love— the Clearwater youth Skate Party at Skateland in Lewiston. My dad works with the owner, Howard Williams at the Railroad. He lets me in free. There's always gobs of kids there.

I'm pretty good going forward, but I can't get the hang of going backward.

"I'll teach you how," Gary promises. He takes my hands and begins to skate backwards as he pulls me to him. "Watch my feet. See it's less work than going forward."

We go around once, twice, then he says, "Your turn." and swings me around. My skate catches his—he falls—I fly over the top of him and land on my left knee. No, no, no! I can't stand the pain. I feel him lifting me under the arms. Howard and Dad rush out to help get me off the rink floor. Oh, this is worse than a black eye. This is worse than slicing my thumb. This is serious.

Howard grabs ice from the concession stand and wraps it in a towel around my leg.

I hear Gary apologizing over and over. "I'm sorry, Sharon. I'm so, so sorry . . ." Mom and Dad take me home.

It's too swollen to walk in the morning even though Mom keeps ice on it all night. I can't go to school. Mom borrows Uncle Pete's crutches. Wednesday, Dad drives me to school and picks me up. People volunteer to carry my books from class to class.

Doctor? No doctor. My family doesn't go to doctors. I've not been to one since I had shots for first grade.

"It will be fine when the swelling goes down." Mom says. Sports are over for me this year.

*   *   *

I have to be able to march in the parade for the school district's May Music Festival. I'm second clarinet. Judy's first. Sandy dropped out of band. Whew!

All schools around Lewiston bring their bands here for competition. They "adjudicate" (that means judge) solos, duets, quintets, and marching in the parade on Saturday. There's a mass band concert Saturday night. It's a really, really big deal. I have to be able to march. I baby my leg, keep it up, walk on it as little as possible and soak it every night. It seems to be getting better. I have two weeks to go. I can do this.

*　　*　　*

This is it. The big May Music Festival. I'm doing a clarinet solo called "The Tribute." I'm nervous. Mrs. Knepper's a great accompanist. Maybe she'll cover up my mistakes. Wow, there's three judges. I didn't expect that. I take deep breaths. A clarinet squawks when you don't have enough air. Don't want that nightmare. The piano starts, I come in and get lost in the song. I don't even notice the judges. Then I sit and wait.

They put their heads together and whisper. It's hard when you know they're talking about you. I can't hear. Heads bob, faces smile and frown and hands go up, down, out. I can't tell if they liked it or not. The clock ticks away.

"Ahem," begins one judge, "Miss Chase, why did you choose to learn the clarinet?"

"Why?" I don't understand what that has to do with my playing. "Why? Well, I like the sound of it. It's soothing and peaceful."

He smiles. "We could hear that. You have a smooth sound. However, your breath control needs work. I suggest you try singing to yourself out loud every day to build your control. You breathe too often. It should be only at the marks. Also, we didn't find much difference between your piano voice and your forte voice. That requires breath control too. We think you'll be an excellent clarinet player once you get your breathing problems taken care of. We're giving you a score of three. Thanks for being brave enough to try this."

A Three? Three? That's terrible. I expected a two and hoped for a one. I guess I'm not very good at this.

I go home disillusioned. I lay out my white pants, white shirt, blue wool jacket and black shoes for the parade tomorrow. At least I know how to march down the street—always look left.

Chapter 44

1954

FLOUNDERING

Sharon

I'm smitten, as my grandma would say. Smitten with a guy named Gary. He's the one I literally fell over roller skating. I'll never forget those six months on crutches.

He's five years older than me. He graduated from Clarkston High last Sunday. Mom, Dad and I went to his graduation.

I let it be known this year; I'm going steady. It keeps guys from asking me out. I don't know how to tell them I can't go 'cause my dad doesn't let me date, dance, or do make-up (I do sneak Tangee lipstick in my purse to put on after I get to school. It makes my lips their brightest natural color.).

Gary doesn't have a job. He lives with his grandma and grandpa. He looks at least twenty-five. He treats me like a queen. He's kind. He's polite. He's thoughtful. He's . . . oh, I think I'm in love. Is this what happened to Patty?

We see each other on Sundays, Wednesday nights, and at youth activities. He doesn't come to Youth for Christ or the Christian Youth Activity Center. Says he has to study. Now he's out of school and I still have two more weeks. He comes to pick me up for lunch every day.

*   *   *

I've gone from euphoria to devastation. Today, Gary told me he's moving to Las Vegas to live with his mom. What? Why? He can't give me an answer.

He only says, "Mom needs me."

I need you too. You're my excuse for not dating, not dancing, not having a boyfriend my age. How can you do this to me? My mind runs helter-skelter.

I've been abandoned. Las Vegas is forever away. Furious, crushed and heart-broken, I cry all night, sleep till noon, and refuse to talk to him when he calls. How dare he do this to me? He's leaves without even saying good-bye.

*   *   *

Susan

I hear Sharon's cries. Can't hide feelings around here if they're let outside the mind. They seep through the no-insulated walls. Crying's good. God'll give her peace. It's her first heartache.

I've never felt comfortable about Gary. He's older. How could I say anything? Tom's five years older than me. I prayed for God to take care of my concern. Now he has. I'll be a listening ear, but not pry. Sharon's private like me. Frustrations, hurts and anger are resolved internally, not shared.

Life's been a game of Upset the Fruit Basket this last year. Family, relationships, church, all topsy turvy. We've been living in a muddle of change.

Church is supposed to be the support when all else fails. I understand why the Johnsons left. Ailene was fragile after their son drowned. She slept most of the time, came to church, played the organ, and left when singing was over. It's all off key. No excitement. No joy. It's not easy to sing with a devastated preacher and his wife. It's right we let them go.

Everything keeps moving along. Two retired preachers take turns speaking. Daddy Nolan's in his nineties, and Brother Cooper's in his eighty's. They don't watch the clock. Sometimes church doesn't get out till one-thirty. You can hear stomachs growling. Older men lead

Wednesday night Bible study. Ladies hold the Women's Missionary Society together. The Hanks keep young people going and Sunday School teachers keep on teaching. We sure miss a fulltime preacher. Praying God sends someone soon. In the meantime, I'm hanging tight to Jesus.

* * *

Tom

Cain't say I enjoy goin' ta church right now. Know I shouldn't say that. It's empty. People goin' through the motions. We need a shepherd. "God, who ya talkin' too. Make um come now."

* * *

Sharon

We're driving in neutral, waiting for God to come up with a plan. We've had three men try out for our preacher. They call them candidates. None were approved by the congregation.

I miss the Johnsons—especially Ailene. She'd invite everybody to stand around the organ and sing after Sunday night services. Choruses, oh how we'd sing choruses—short, great beat, and fun. She taught me how to play the organ. Coordinating two feet, hands on two keyboards and all the levers is a challenge. We go early Sunday nights so I can practice like she's still here. If they ever come back, I'll surprise her with how hard I've worked.

In this morning's service, they announce, "Next Sunday, a man named Edwin C. Ogle from Kansas is coming to try out for our preacher."

Ogle? The pastor at Moscow, Idaho is named Ogle. Wonder if they're related. Rev. Ogle and his wife, Charlcie, are Mom and Dad's age. They have a son my age named David. Hmm. Sounds good. Their two older boys are married and settled in Kansas. Is this the preacher God's going to send us?

*   *   *

Susan

As far as I'm concerned, they can quit having candidates. Reverend Ogle's the real thing. So's his wife. This tall, grey-haired man speaks with soft authority, knows his Bible, and has experience in a large congregation. His four-foot-nine wife is cute as a button and a real firecracker. God told me this is the family he wants here. Tom said the same thing. Hope the people at church hear that too. We vote next Sunday.

*   *   *

Sharon

Yea, we've got a new preacher. They'll be moving into the parsonage in two weeks so David can start school. Girls in the youth group are especially excited to have a new, good-looking guy around. More guys attract more girls and vise-versa. I see great things happening here.

*   *   *

Ninth grade flies by. Scads of homework, youth group, Youth for Christ, and the Activity Center consume my time.

By the way, we love the Ogles. She insists we call her Mom Ogle and our preacher, Pop Ogle. That's what David calls them. We're like their adopted kids. They love us.

Chapter 45

1954

CAMP

Sharon

School's out. I'm frantically picking berries. I need seventeen dollars before July to pay for Camp Wooten. Never been to a youth camp before.

Mom Ogle says, "Oh sweety, it's nothing like you've ever experienced. For five days, you sleep in a cabin, eat in the dining hall, play games, study, hike, have campfires. You'll love it."

I need ten more dollars.

"Sharon," Mom calls, "There's a Mrs. Wagner on the phone. She's asking if you'd like a job for a week."

"Hello, this is Sharon," I say into the black receiver.

"Hi, Sharon. Your name was given to me by a friend who thought you'd be good with my three-year-old son, Bobby. My baby's due soon. I need help with dishes, washing clothes, vacuuming, and keeping Bobby entertained. My husband's a farmer and can't take time off. I need someone to help for a week or so. Would you be interested?"

"Yes." I try to keep excitement out of my voice. "I can do that. Do I need to bring anything?"

"Oh, no. Bobby has lots of toys. You'll need to fix lunch for him. He likes sandwiches, fruit, and cookies. I'd like you to come around eight o'clock and leave around five o'clock. Jack gets home around six.

I'll call you after the baby arrives to let you know when I'll be coming home."

"That will be fine. Thank you." I hang up, thinking I should be able to handle this. A three- year-old can't be too hard. I can dust, vacuum, get lunch. The biggest problem will be the clothes. I have vivid memories of my failure at the ironing job.

The day after we finish the last of the berries, Mrs. Wagner calls. She wants me to start tomorrow morning.

Dad drops me off on his way to work. Wow, you should see this house. It's huge; has two floors, a basement, and a garage. I guess farmers make more money than railroad workers.

The Misses looks tired. The baby's tiny. She'll take care of her. Thank goodness.

She shows me where I'll find everything I need. I don't have to go to the second floor for anything. I'm in charge of Bobby, cleaning the play room, kitchen, dining room, living room and bathroom on the main floor. The room where Bobby's toys are has a television. I'm fascinated. I've heard about them, but never seen one before. In the basement, oh dear, in the basement is the washer, dryer and a huge Mangle iron.

She says, "Use the Mangle to iron the sheets, table clothes and my husband's pants. The rest you can use a regular iron." I nod and wonder why they keep inventing fancy new things for ironing. I'll have to ask how to run it when it comes time.

"Bobby," Mrs. Wagner calls. "Bobby."

"What?" a small voice answers from upstairs.

"Come. I want you to meet Sharon. She's going to help us for a few days."

A toe-head boy bounces into the room, screeches to a halt, and hides behind his mother.

"Hi, Bobby," I reach out my hand. "I'm Sharon. Can you show me around your playroom? What's your favorite toy?" He creeps out and runs into the playroom. I follow. The Bobby part of this job's going to be easy. It's the Mangle that has me worried.

*   *   *

Everything about this job is hunky dory. I've been here six days. Misses is getting stronger every day. The baby cries a lot. Yesterday she showed me how to run the wash machine and dryer. The washer's completely different than Mom's. I've never seen a dryer before. Both are easy. I read the buttons and pushed the right ones.

Today, I Mangle and iron in the basement. She demonstrates a sheet then leaves. I do the other ironing first, procrastinating the dreaded new-fangled machine. Finally, I have to tackle it. Let's just say, it has the proper name—mangel. It was a mangled mess. I had to do everything at least twice. I did get better the more I used it. She laughed and said she had a hard time with it too sometimes. She's a nice lady.

Two more days and Mrs. Wagner gives me a twenty dollar bill and says thanks for all the help. Now I have enough to go to camp plus money to spend at the snack bar.

*   *   *

Mom Ogle was right. There's nothing like youth camp. Three meals a day, devotions, Bible study, baseball, volley ball, wading in the creek, catching crayfish, hiking, campfire at night, singing, new friends, a young preacher, and not much sleep because of giggles.

Our camp preacher is Wendell Wallace. We love him. He's there all the time and does everything with us. He's a little guy with dark brown skin. I grew up a few miles from the Nez Perce reservation. I've had oodles of brown friends. Wendall's different though. He gets so excited when he preaches, he almost jumps right over the pulpit. He's good friends with God. He has a conversation with Him even while he's preaching. His words light God-sparks in the darkest places of my mind. I can tell you right now, camp's a place to grow closer to God. Wish I could stay here for a month. It seems like we just got here.

It's time to leave. Pastor Wendell calls it, "going from a mountain top experience to the deep, dark valley of life." He's right. I'm full of my most happy ever. I dread going back to the valley.

Chapter 46

IN THE VALLEY

August 1954

Tom

Two years ago, I gave my heart ta God. I came out a new man. No more swearin', no smokin', not gettin' mad, not wantin' ta hear bad things.

There's this guy at work named Jack who's got it in fer me. He's made life miserable ever since I told him why I'm different. Calls me names, cracks dirty jokes makin' sure I hear them. He tries ta break me every chance he gits. Makes him mad I don't act back at him. Can't do it. Just gonna trust Jesus to give me the power to love 'em.

I work in the round house at the railroad changin' flat tires on rail cars. Yep, that happens 'cause of fast stops, wear and tear, and goin' down steep grades. Tires are 'bout three inches thick so we redo 'em on a wheel lathe if there's 'nough metal left.

It takes two people to jack up the car, unscrew the tires, heat it up in a hot fire and lift it on the lathe. I'm stuck with Jack as my tire partner.

Today we're workin' on an old flat car. It's been in here a lot this last year. Prob'ly should change the whole wheel track, but the company says it costs too much. The bolts ain't comin' off easy. I'm workin' on one side, Jack is gettin' at the other side. I hear him swearin'up a storm 'bout one he cain't get loose.

"If you'll give a minute, I'll come get it," I say.

"Ol' man Chase, ya think you're so much better than me. Just wantin' to show me God's power aren't ya. Well, forget it. I can do it without God. Ya just stay on your side, ol' man." He yells. He grunts, groans, changes to a bigger wrench. I can hear his swearin', gettin' more furious.

I loosen my tire and start rollin' it 'round the flat bed. I see Jack's red face starin' at me like a ragin' bull. His wrench comes flyin' 'cross the flat car and hits me in the back of the head. That's all I remember.

* * *

Susan

"Hello," I answer on the third ring. It's the railroad. Something's happened to Tom. They're bringing him home. I'm speechless. "All right," is all I can say. I call Sharon home from Jensen's house.

We sit and wait. Minutes drag. A black car pulls into the driveway. We dash out to help.

Tom's dazed but able to walk. The driver and I help him into the house.

"Can you tell me what happened?" I ask the man.

"No, can't tell you. Jack came running into the office saying Tom's passed out and needs help . . . and something about an old geezer like him shouldn't be allowed to work. Don't understand it. Isn't Tom only forty-nine?'

I nod. Look at Tom. He opens his mouth, but can't speak. The man gives him a pat on the shoulder and leaves.

"Do you want to lay down on the bed?" I ask my pale husband. He answers with a small shake of his head. Sharon and I help him sit in his green chair.

"Get him a glass of water," I tell Sharon. He sips it slowly. It's hot. August is always in the triple digits. He needs water. His shirt is soaked and dirty. Sweat pours down his face.

"Get the fan out of your room and I'll get a cold cloth." We scramble to make him more comfortable.

An hour later, Tom's breathing more normal. Color's coming back to his face. He raises a trembling hand and points to the back of his neck. I move the collar of his green work shirt and gasp. There a red, tennis ball size knot at the bottom of his head. I run to get ice. Thank goodness I filled all the ice trays this morning. He winces at the cold and closes his eyes.

We sit on the sofa and wait, and wait, and wait. God what should I do? I don't know what happened. You take care of us in dark times. I must trust you.

*　　*　　*

Sharon

Dad's always been strong. Sometimes too strong. Dad took charge of our family when he let God take charge of his life. I have to admit I've been a bit miffed about that. He changed the rules. He demands, "Do as I say." His old-fashioned ideas about being a girl in high school are embarrassing and irritating. Sometimes I'm humiliated; even down-right angry. I know what it says in the Bible, "Honor your father and mother." I admit there are times when I don't like my dad. I keep my feelings to myself. It wouldn't be right to let them out of my mouth.

Right now, watching Dad unable to speak, shakes me hard. I never thought about Dad not being Dad anymore. What if he never speaks again? What if he can't work? What if he can't take care of the house, the land, the animals . . . what if? I'm a jumble of emotions.

When I came from my mountain-top camp back to the valley, I had no idea how dark the valley might be. Mom said I was ready to walk my own bridge. I don't think so. The stone of unexpected events is missing. I'm falling through. I want to hop back to Mom's bridge.

Chapter 47

A Nightmare

Sharon

We manage to get Dad in bed. Mom and I nibble leftover chicken and fresh prunes. I'm not hungry. My throat closes each time I swallow.

"You must eat, Sharon," She tells me. "We need to keep strong for your dad."

I can't tell her how scared I am. I don't want her to worry about me. She needs to focus on Dad. Concern lines her eyes. Calm envelopes her body. I know she uses silence to talk to Jesus, her Rock.

The evening passes at caterpillar speed. Mom checks his sleep, his breathing, his shaking. August heat swelters our little house as temperatures above one hundred degrees flood through the poorly insulated walls. Small windows open to six-inch height, a fan is in the window, cold wet clothes help cool Dad's body. The odor of over-heated bodies is punctuated by the smell of fear.

"Let's try to get some rest," Mom suggests.

I'm amazed at how exhausted I've grown in the quiet tension. I've been sleeping on a blanket in the cooler back yard. Not tonight. I must stay alert, ready to help if needed.

"Good night, Mama," I give her hand a squeeze. "Call me if you need me." At that moment, I wish I could throw my arms around her and make all this go away. Mom's not a huggy person. I know my wish has no power to make this disappear. I fling myself on the bed and talk silently to God.

*   *   *

"AUGGGGHHHH..OOOOORRR!" A horrendous sound stabs me awake.

Mama screams my name. "Sharon, SHARON, HELP ME! COME HELP ME!"

I bounce off the bed and into their bedroom. Dad's gagging, choking, uncontrolled in a nightmarish uproar. His body twists like demon possession. His wild arms hit Mom. His feet stomp the air.

"What shall I do?" I scream over the din.

"Get a washcloth!" I dash in and out of the bathroom.

"Help me get it between his teeth. He's trying to swallow his tongue . . . he's choking . . ." She gives directions and explanation. "Hold his arms so he doesn't hit." She somehow works the cloth between his lips and over his tongue while I cling with all my might to hold down his arms and body. He's unbelievably strong. A half hour ticks away on the alarm clock before the horrible sounds stop, his body relaxes and his breathing becomes steady, although ragged and raspy.

"I'm calling the doctor." Mom rushes to the living room and dials Dr. Stover. It's 2:00 a.m. It doesn't matter. He'll come. He came when Mom had food poisoning. He came when I had strep throat. He's a good man. He'll come.

I watch Dad, and pray. His eyes flutter open. He looks confused. He's pillowcase-white. Sweat glows in the lamplight. He looks at me, eyes not seeing.

I speak softly. "I'm here, Daddy. I love you. Just relax."

Dr. Stover arrives in fifteen minutes. He listens to Mom in the living room then comes into the bedroom.

"Hi, Tom," he greets, "I hear you've had a rough night." He sits in the chair by the bed and begins to explain what has happened. "Tom, you've suffered a Grand Mal Seizure. I need to know what happened to cause this."

Mom and I stand in the doorway and watch the doctor work his magic. As he talks, Dad begins to focus, breathe quietly and spits out disjointed sentences. He tells about the hit on the back of his head. Dr. Stover turns him on his side and examines the swelling.

"My, my, that's quite a lump you have there, Tom. Let's try having you sleep on your side to take the pressure off." The doctor digs in his bag and gives Dad a shot to help him sleep. "I recommend you don't go to work tomorrow. You're going to be extremely tired. It won't be safe to work around machines."

He looks at Mom and me. "I have some instructions for you in case this happens again. First off, stay calm. Don't try to restrain him. Don't try to put anything in his mouth. The seizure will eventually calm down. Be sure he's in a safe place where he won't fall or hurt himself."

Oh, man. I thought. We did all the wrong things. Thanks, God, for saving my dad from our ignorance.

*   *   *

Days are calm. Dad's weak, but able to speak. He takes naps in his big green chair. Doctor Stover writes a note to the railroad about his condition.

It says, "Can't go back to work without a doctor's release."

Night after night, we contend with seizures. I go to bed, but not to sleep. I wait for Dad's snoring to stop. The breathing stops. I brace myself, ready for the horrendous sounds of seizure. It comes without fail.

How can we live with this nightmare? Dad's exhausted. Mom's walking in her sleep. I can't even think about school starting next week.

*   *   *

I'm a sophomore. First thing I learn is the meaning of: wise fool. Well, that's certainly not me. I have a good head on my shoulders. My mother taught me to make wise choices, be kind to people, love Jesus, and do my best.

I'm excited about getting to take driver education. Aunt Neen's been taking me out on farmer roads to teach me how to drive her new Chevy Bel Air. She's a great teacher and her car's so cool. Now I have to get a learner's permit.

"Sorry," the clerk stares at me. "You have to be fourteen to be issued a learner's permit."

"I'll be fourteen by the time I finish driver education. You can have a daytime license in Idaho when you're fourteen. I'm a sophomore, and I've been driving farmer roads with my aunt for five months. I need a permit so I can take the class and learn to drive safely," I argue.

The lady looks at my dad. "Is this true?"

"Yes," Dad looks at me and grins. "She started 1st grade when she's five."

She gives in. We pay my two dollars. I walk out with a learner's permit.

"Sure glad Neen's teached ya ta drive. I'd never have the patience," Dad whispered to me on the way out of the courthouse.

Class starts the next day after regular school hours. Not the driving, only studying the driver's manual. Our instructors are Jimmy Asker and Sgt. Ferguson. Great guys with a sense of humor. You'd have to for this job.

They give us a schedule for the semester. Oh, look at this. We're going to learn to change a flat tire, put on chains, and learn how to handle the car in snow. Whoa, and we get to drive up the Lewiston hill. That road's a twister. I hear the man who designed it went crazy after he finished it. Hm.

My other classes are demanding: English (every year, English), Algebra, Biology, American History, Latin, and PE. The class I adore is choir. Mr. Harris really knows his stuff. I enjoy it much more than band.

Our nightmare at home hasn't changed much. Dad still has seizures three or four times a week. I've learned to listen for two hours after he goes to sleep. If he makes it past two hours, I can go to sleep.

He's not gone back to work. The doctor won't release him because he works around machinery. I don't understand. He only has these things at night. Never in the day time. He probably wouldn't be much good on the job. He's wiped out the next day.

Sometimes it seems a seizure happens when he's upset with me. We argue, I stay out with friends too long, or forget to tell him about something. He gets angry easy. It's a tiptoeing life. Hard to live. I want to spread my wings—become independent. He has a seizure. I dive into deep guilt.

*   *   *

The railroad sends Dad to the railroad hospital in Missoula, Montana. He has to catch a train out of Spokane, over a hundred miles away. He drives up, boards the train, and we wave him off. I drive Mom and me back home. It's my first long distance trip. I get to drive the Lewiston hill before anyone else in my class. I'm only thirteen.

Sunday afternoon, I drive back to Spokane and pick Dad up at Reverend First's house where he's staying after they picked him up from the depot Saturday night. Mom's my navigator. I don't know much about maps yet.

*   *   *

Susan

"Mom, does my driving make you nervous?" Sharon asks several times.

"No, you're a good driver," I assure her. She is. In fact, she's more aware of cars, takes less chances and watches more around her than Tom does. No fear. God's timing is perfect so we could make this trip.

"What did the doctors say?" I ask Tom as we settle in the car. He insists on driving.

"Let me git outa this heavy traffic, then talk," he responds. I know he's nervous by the way he grips the wheel and drives slower than usual. It bothers him to turn his head so he has to rely on the mirrors. That makes me nervous. Once we get on the highway, he replies.

"Hrumph." he grunts. "They don't know no-more than me. They x-rayed, poked, prodded, and watched me sleep for a week. Four seizures. Said nothing made it happen. Gave me pills ta relax. Huh?

They just shrugged and said I gotta live with it. I don't wanna live with it. Gotta git back to work. Waste of time."

Silence rides with us the next two hours as we each try to process what the future will look like. Jesus' persistent whisper nudges my mind: *I will never leave you nor forsake you.*

Chapter 48

A SEASON OF PAINFUL GROWTH

Sharon

It's the first time in three years Mom's family's been all together on Christmas. Patty and Al come from Texas with a tiny addition named Debbie. We spend Christmas Day at Edna and Pete's. Today it's ham and scalloped potatoes (sure glad I didn't have to pluck a goose), and four kinds of pies. Aunt Edna's famous for her pies. Of course, we all bring food. Mom always makes two kinds of potato salad, with and without onions, and her famous baked beans.

Even though it's good we're together, tension fogs the air. Everyone's careful not to say the wrong thing; not to show their disappointments and hurts about how life's turned out. It's not like the old days of bantering and teasing and freedom to be ourselves. Something says, this is it. Family will never be the same. It isn't a Merry Christmas.

* * *

Christmas break's too short. Sleeping in is delightful ... especially when we've had a hard night with Dad. I feel rested for the first time since August. I've come to accept our family's life in this dark valley. I work hard at being a good daughter; not rocking the boat.

Yet the break is too long. I love learning. I miss the brain challenges. I miss being with my friends. To be honest, I miss getting out of the house. We've not gone anywhere these two weeks, except to church. No events, no parties, no extra youth activities . . . not even youth group or the Activity Center. It's supposed to be family time.

*   *   *

I'm up and eager to catch my bus. I grab my books, new supplies and my bag that holds my clean gym clothes and scrubbed, white tennis shoes.

The bus is loaded with laughter and chatter. Excitement spills out the closed windows. I'm first off the bus. I rush to my locker, deposit my load, and hustle to the cafeteria to join RD, Anna Lou, Patty, and Nancy. We haven't seen each other for two weeks. There's catching up to do.

The bell for first class rings all too soon. The whirlwind of school sweeps us down the halls forcing us to put order back in life. It's a contented feeling. Classes blend smoothly. For my first day back, I have hot lunch. Mmm, my favorite. Turkey gravy over mashed potatoes with green beans and fruit salad. I gobble it down as I listen to my friends' continued stories about vacation. There goes that bell again. I'm off to PE. We're starting basketball today.

Warm ups get your muscles ready for the game. We do stretches, lunges, crossovers and jumping jacks.

"One more," Mrs. Kytonen says, "This is a new one to limber up your knees and hips. Pretend you're a ballet dancer. Stand with your heels about six inches apart. Good. Now, point your toes out and form a V with your feet." Some of us loose our balance and have to try again. "Next, bend your knees slowly down. That's it. Slowly so you don't lose your bal . . ."

There is a loud crack in my left knee. My knee cap falls to the outside of my leg. I fall to the floor and scream. "No, No. Not that knee again." Our teacher rushes to my side, to check my leg. I see alarm on her face as she sends Amy to the office for help.

"Stay still," she whispers.

"Can I lay down?" The world spins. Someone's dimmed the lights. I feel her lay me on the gym floor and tuck something under my head.

I hear nothing else until Mr. Hill's voice says, "It's going to be okay, Sharon. We're taking you to the doctor."

"We don...don...'t go ... to ..." I feel myself lifted by four men, carried out the back door and carefully placed in the back seat of a car. The throbbing is unbearable. It's a short ride. People rush to help me into a wheel chair. I catch sight of my mis-configured knee and vomit to the side of the chair.

"Sorry," is all I can get out.

They wheel me straight into Dr. Douglas's patient room. He wears a serious frown when he sees my knee.

"Let's get her on the table," he orders. "Lie flat, Sharon. This isn't going to be pleasant. Nurse hold her hand. Try to relax. It will help the muscles slacken and release their hold on your knee cap."

A nurse stands to my left side and leans over a little so I can't see what's happening.

"It's going to be just fine, sweetheart." She distracts me. "Dr. Douglas knows what he's doing. Tell me about what happened?"

"I was doing this new . . ." Crack and a sharp pain shoots up my leg interrupting what I saying. Tears stream.

"OW!" I yelp.

"Now, we need to get x-rays to see the damage." The doctor orders.

I look at my leg. The kneecap's back in place. It's swelling, like it did when I fell roller skating. My poor knee.

"Can I call my folks?" I manage to get out.

"Not until we x-ray. I want to be able to tell them the whole story," Doctor Douglas replies as I'm wheeled out of the room to a huge machine and black bench. They lay me on the bench. The machine hums and clicks at least a dozen times before I'm wheeled out.

The nurse brings me a glass of water and a pill. "Here, sweetheart, this will help the pain." She startles me with a cold bag on my knee.

It's almost time for me to be getting home. Mom and Dad will worry when I don't get off the bus. I've been here three hours. I'm stewing. How am I going to get home? I've missed my bus. The door opens and my folks walk in. Whew.

"Am I glad to see you!" I cry. "I'm sorry, I'm so, so sorry. I wasn't even doing anything except a dumb new exercise. I . . . I ..." I burst into sobs. They both hug and hold me until the tears stop.

Dr. Douglas comes in with a fist full of black pictures. He puts them against a lit-up window, shakes hands with Mom and Dad, and introduces himself.

"These are pictures of Sharon's knee. It looks like it's been injured before," he begins.

The three of us nod.

"Roller skating, eighth grade," I say softly.

"Must have been a hard hit," he continues. "There's all kinds of loose cartilage floating around in your knee joint. That's the stuff that softens the movement of your knee joint and protects the bone. Your knee cap looks badly damaged too. I need to do surgery right now to clean out the floaters and stabilize the joint, or you'll never be able to walk properly again."

My eyes dart to Mom and Dad. I shake my head. No. I can't put them through this. Dad's not well, laid off work, no income. Surgery costs a fortune. How can I put them in debt just so I can walk right? No! I can't do this. My mountain-top camp experience caves around me into agonizing blackness. I'm confused, terrified, bombarded with a jumble of disconnected thoughts.

I look at Mom. Her eyes are closed. I've watched her do this many times. She's listening to Jesus, re-building her shaking bridge. Silence waits for an answer.

Can I do this? I close my eyes. *I tried to build my own bridge. I thought I could hop back to Mom's if I fall apart. I can't. I have to ask for help. Can't do it alone. I'm scared, I'm full of guilt. I'm anxious. Help!*

Paul's words to Timothy whisper through the smell of rubbing alcohol, the sounds of jagged breathing and the tension of a distressing decision.

> *"For God hath not given us the spirit of fear, but of*
> *power and of love and of a sound mind."*

My eyes pop open. Mom and Dad nod at me.

I look at Dr. Douglas and stutter out, "O… o…kay, let's do it."

I've crossed Mom's bridge. The Rock of unexpected events has been positioned in my bridge. It's safe to travel.

www.ingramcontent.com/pod-product-compliance
Lightning Source LLC
La Vergne TN
LVHW091251080426
835510LV00007B/208